Canoeing Basics for Beginners

Ray and Moraima Ovington

Stackpole Books

Canoeing Basics for Beginners

Copyright © 1984 by Ray and Moraima Ovington

Published by
STACKPOLE BOOKS
Cameron and Kelker Streets
P.O. Box 1831
Harrisburg, PA 17105

Selected illustrations by David Hettle.

Printed in the U.S.A.

Library of Congress Cataloging in Publication Data
Ovington, Ray.
    Canoeing basics for beginners.

I. Canoes and canoeing. I. Ovington, Moraima.
II. Title.
GV783.093   1984   797.1'22   83-17973
ISBN 0-8117-2212-0

Contents

PART ONE

Basic Equipment

Dave, a very good friend of ours, turned seventy a few years ago. He's never had the use of his legs, yet he has probably canoed over more waters than anyone we know. Whenever we can catch him for a trip, he acts as stern paddler and guide. Ask him about a specific water south of the Arctic circle and he's been there.

A couple we have known for years, now in their early seventies, are relatively new at canoeing and are our constant companions. Not even a strong north wind will keep them and their cameras from the river. We all know how youngsters take happily to canoeing at summer camps and resorts. We can certainly vouch for middle-aged canoeists — hunters, campers, fishermen, naturalists — since we have passed through that age bracket to senior citizenship.

So, don't get the idea you are too young, too middle-aged, or too old to enjoy canoeing fully as a pastime, as recreation, or as healthy exercise. Best of all, canoeing on camping trips is the perfect outdoor experience — a time when the generation gap disappears.

Having instructed canoeists of all ages, as camp counselors to our good friends, we have had the opportunity to learn the needs that arise in instructing. We have observed the typical reactions of beginners during their first hours in a canoe.

Here in this book of basics is the distillation of many years of experiencing all kinds of canoes and equipment as they have developed through space age technology and all types of water and conditions afloat.

There is so much rural and wilderness water to explore in our great country — endless uncrowded waterways, lakes, rivers, streams, and even ponds — just waiting nearby for you. Your canoe will glide you into places boats will not (or should not) go. It will bring you there silently, free from gas fumes, so you can experience the essence of the great outdoors the way the Indians and pioneers knew it.

So, join us now. Point your bow outward and paddle into the sunrise of a gratifying experience.

1

What It Takes to Canoe Well

A lot of good things have happened to canoes and the sport of canoeing over the past thousand years – and especially since the 1950s. The variety of hull designs is still basically the same, but the materials developed by modern space-age techniques for making a canoe have revolutionized the canoe into a safer, more responsive craft.

The result is a whole new world of aquatic enjoyment. Canoeing, with its near brother kayaking, has become one of the biggest industries in the recreational field. Today millions can afford a first-class, well-designed, stable, safe craft to carry them on the waters of a nearby creek or lake, a large river, and yes, even a broad wind-swept lake or tortuous white water falls and rapids.

It all started perhaps a thousand years ago, and the American Indian is responsible. The canoe was a necessary invention to carry him where he wanted to go on the water in a craft that could bring his needed equipment, duffle, and supplies.

Not having a manufacturing plant at his disposal, the American Indian fashioned the first canoes from nature using wood, bark, and animal skins. He had no metal or plastics. He must have had a keen

Figure 1. Typical canoe bows showing the gradual evolution from the earliest days of the birch bark shapes when the Indians designed their bows high and handsome and placed their identification marks prominently. The first white man–made and marketed canoes were made of wood planks and ribs and covered on the outside with canvas. Note the lowered peaks. The more workhorse guide models lowered the peaks still further, and today the modern racing and fast water canoes have hardly any rise other than the peaks which are rockered sometimes. Still more modern are the completely flat bows, called "banana boats," that look more like boats than canoes.

eye for design of the canoe hull, because the hull has been changed very little since those early times. Certainly, he made several models, types, lengths, widths, and depths to give him a fast means of travel and to carry a heavy cargo for all his warring needs. When the first white men invaded his country, the canoe was the Indian's salvation. It often meant an edge on his adversaries since they neither had access to his craft nor could they build a canoe themselves.

Our first pioneers' canoes inspired the models that became indispensable during the early days of exploration. Those models are still used today for scientific research in remote areas where other types of craft cannot go.

The first white man–made canoes were developed by companies such as Old Town in Maine, and Indians were the designers and manufacturers. Only a generation ago the planked and ribbed canoe that was covered with canvas came into being, and that type of manufacture remained until the coming of fiberglass, various plastics, and aluminum. Today Old Town and a few of the pioneers in constructing wood strip canoes keep the tradition alive for those who can appreciate such a work of art and can afford it. The latest development in this class of canoe is the do-it-yourself strip-built kits that are available for those who enjoy the ultimate in craftsmanship.

Whether your idea of canoeing is the casual use of a canoe in a nearby lake or river, or you are in the market for a canoe that will

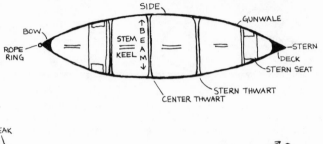

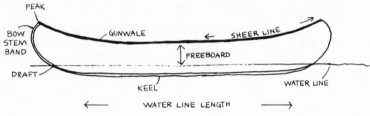

Figure 2. Canoe nomenclature.

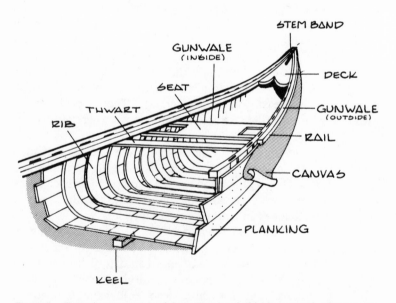

Figure 3. Typical construction of the stripped and ribbed canoe either bare or canvas covered. The wood canoes, painted today with a hard, clear glass covering revealing the grain and workmanship of the wood, are beautiful to behold as well as costly. The strip canoe without ribs is either covered with canvas or finished in clear glass.

take hard use as a plaything or even harder use in constant travel under all kinds of conditions, there is a canoe for your needs — one specifically designed to perform and to last. Canoes have their limitations just as any other craft, but they also have many advantages over conventional boats. Thanks to human ingenuity and a constant desire to improve designs and materials, the canoe is still undergoing more subtle development, dictated by the demands of an increasing variety of recreational uses.

Fortunately there are hundreds of canoe makers across the land who have been following their own instincts as to the perfect canoe for their region. A recent issue of *Canoe* magazine lists over one thousand recognized designs; there will probably be many more in the years to come. (A complete list of canoe manufacturers is in appendix A.) Many manufacturers list more than one model and style with several lengths in order to accommodate your needs. The major canoe builders have been around for a long time and, despite competition from local builders, have carved a niche in the trade that assures you both quality manufacturing and reasonable guarantees. Standards in the canoe-building business are high, and dealers are constantly upgrading their services.

The simple canoe paddle has also undergone some major variations (see chapter 6). Accessories such as cartop carriers, lifesaving jackets and cushions, containers for lunches and cameras, and other day cruise equipment and canoe camping gear have also been improved. It is hard for this generation to realize that oldsters never had plastics of any kind.

As the demand for accessible waters has grown, organizations of canoe outfitters, clubs, and associations have grown. Most offer rental canoes and a complete line of gear for their particular stretches of lakes or streams.

When you step aboard your canoe, you will be following in the footsteps of the early Indian. Your modern, technically sound, and virtually maintenance free canoe will take you silently, efficiently, and carefully wherever you want to go. Take your camera to record the beauty of nature or, if you like to camp, store your duffle afloat and enjoy the wilderness by the waterside.

There are an increasing number of us who enjoy racing, the excitement of running white water rapids, and even taking the canoe into the surf. Whether it be a canoe that you will use only casually for

NATIONAL ASSOCIATION OF CANOE LIVERIES AND OUTFITTERS

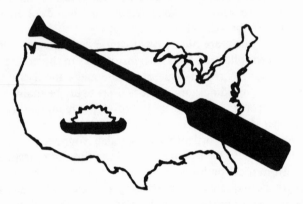

Figure 4. The NACLO logo. A complete listing of NACLO outfitters is in appendix B.

your lakeside dock or a canoe for performance, there is one waiting for you. And there are thousands of miles of streams, rivers, lakes, bayous, ponds, and hundred-mile-long waterways in the United States and the southern provinces of Canada where you can wet your paddle.

2

Rent or Buy?

Many people, especially those who have not yet joined the boating clan, hesitate to take the plunge and buy a canoe because they are skittery about the "tippy" canoe. They would like to try canoeing without making a large initial investment. Unless they know someone who owns a canoe and is willing to take them out for a ride and teach them the rudiments of paddling, they may stay on the shore for the rest of their lives and miss the thrills of paddling. Fortunately many young people who go to summer camps are instructed in canoe handling and become experts in one summer. They are converts. But those who have not had this opportunity or do not live near water where there are canoes available are sometimes reluctant to commit themselves.

One answer is to rent a canoe from a state park livery, a canoe rental service, or even a dealer who sells canoes. While many who initially rent later choose to own their canoe, some prefer to rent. Some may not have a place to house a canoe when it is not in use. Others may find it difficult to hoist a canoe onto a car top or may be afraid to drive their car with a canoe on the top. Renting is easy because there are no maintenance problems and no fear of theft. Renting is also convenient. Even those who own their canoes will often decide to leave them at home when driving a long distance to a river or lake; they know that the livery at the site will have good canoes and all the needed accessories.

Most members of the National Association of Canoe Liveries and Outfitters (NACLO) offer the added feature of put-in and pick-up at the end of a run—a great convenience unless two cars of canoeists go together. If you are interested in running a specific stretch of river from highway A to highway B, how are you going to do it with only one car, unless you plan to paddle back upstream to your original landing?

The cost of a really fine canoe starts at $300 and usually runs into the $500-plus bracket; you can take fifty daylong canoe trips at approximately $10 a throw. During this time you will get to know the subtleties of paddling and safety afloat. Your mate or friend might become bored with the idea, or the youngsters might prefer their space-age games to canoeing. There are a lot of influences that can compete with canoeing within the family. And let's face it— canoeing isn't for everybody. Some prefer a fast outboard skiff, or surfing, or one of a hundred other forms of recreation.

Canoe renters have on hand the most practical canoes for both beginners and experts. They know that their canoes will be put to hard and sometimes damaging use, so they have a stock of safe and sturdy canoes, paddles, and accessories. Renting their equipment will help you determine what to buy if you decide to take the plunge with your checkbook.

Once the virus has taken, and you, or you and your friends or family like the idea, make sure you have a place to store a canoe, either on a dock, in a shed, or hanging from the ceiling of a garage.

Canoes that are well cared for hold their value more than any other boating craft. Recently, I sold my 17-foot Grumman that was eight years old for sixty dollars less than I paid for it. A good canoe is an investment as long as you care for it.

3

Buying Secondhand

If you are careful, you can successfully buy a secondhand canoe, usually at a nominal price compared to buying a new one off the display floor. You should know the reasonable price on the going market and take into consideration the exact condition of the canoe you have in mind.

If you are not in a hurry, spend some time looking at several canoes advertised in the classifieds of your local paper or visit a canoe livery or state park renting office; both sell their canoes after some years of use. Also, some people become tired of their canoes. Retirees may sell out; death or moving away may be factors in the sale of a canoe. There are countless reasons for selling a canoe. You can often get quite a bargain, especially if the owner is not aware of the market value of his craft.

If you have outgrown a canoe, sell it and buy another secondhand unless you have the money to buy one new. Chances are that if and when you wish to resell a canoe, if you have kept it in reasonably good condition, you will be able to realize almost what you paid for it – or sometimes even more.

A general price gauge for a secondhand canoe, assuming the condition is good, is about 50 percent of the list price. Since prices have risen drastically in the past years, you can figure on the current price of a similar or identical canoe as of today, and then mark it down as secondhand about 50 percent, except for aluminum which holds its value better than others (see chapter 4). Of course if you are looking at a canvas-covered wood construction canoe, it is a collector's item. Depending on the condition, it will be unreasonable as a second-hand purchase — somewhat like the outrageous prices of antique cars. Once in a while, however, you may run across such a collector's item with the person selling it unaware of its value. If you do, grab it, even if you use it very little. Ten years from now it will be priceless.

Thoroughly inspect the prospective canoe for bends, bent keel, uneven sides — scratches, gouges, dents — and leaks — the general "look." Has it been patched or repaired? Is there any rot or soggy spots showing? It is advisable to have an expert canoeist present to look for problems you would not spot. If you buy from a dealer, find out about his reputation and any guarantee he may offer.

4

Selecting a Canoe

Ah, the fun and the frustration of shopping for a canoe. If you are the type of person who wants to compare price in relation to quality of manufacture, type of material, and length, weight, and hull design, you will thoroughly enjoy sitting at your fireside reading all the canoe promotion folders. They are primarily "sell" pieces, and each states that their canoe is the best. Beware. It may be that their best is not your best.

It would be great if you could test ride all of them and then decide on the right canoe for the waters on which you will generally use the canoe. Whether you will use it as a solo canoe, will have a constant companion in the bow, or will be carrying an extra passenger on your outings are points to consider.

You can't test ride every canoe, but some dealers have canoes that they will loan you for a trial run; they will often accompany you, especially if you are a beginner, to instruct you, to explain the advantages of the canoes they sell, and to offer comparisons with other models and styles. Actually, if you are a beginner unused to the subtleties of handling a canoe and recognizing its response, the test run is of little value, even though you may think it would be. Even the experts have difficulty in choosing one canoe over another unless they have a specific type of canoe in mind and the designs are radically different.

Look at the catalogues and perhaps test paddle a few canoes. Better yet, have a friend take you out in his canoe or rent one from the local livery. Then you will begin to have some perspective and a list of comparisons that will help you ascertain just what you want in a canoe according to the uses you have planned.

This all sounds quite pat. Suppose, for example, all you want is a canoe to paddle around the local lake. Almost any canoe in the right size and load capacity will fulfill this need. But then, perhaps, the canoe bug really bites and you find yourself wanting to travel to more distant rivers or lakes that offer a wider variety of conditions; the plain old "do anything" canoe may be found wanting. Or perhaps you want to get into racing or sailing or you find white water canoeing fascinating. This may call for another type of canoe later on. It is possible that you may want a canoe that is lighter to portage and lift on and off your car. Hundreds of possibilities for trading in the old for something new and better may arise over the years as you become an expert canoeist.

As a starter, you will discover that basic recreational canoes are generally from 15 to 18 feet in length. The 10s, 12s, and 13s are generally made for solo canoeing, and the 20s are for specific, heavy-duty wilderness travel. The basic canoe is double ended. The bow lines and stern lines are identical. You can paddle them in either direction. The best way is to have the stern paddler in the stern since the seat is placed nearer to the canoe's end affording a better steering position. If you are canoeing solo and into a wind or high wave condition it is better to paddle from the bow seat facing the stern of the canoe. The bow seat is set a bit farther back from the bow for better balance and more bow in front. Usually there are three thwarts, or crossbars, that hold the canoe together for strength — the first just behind the bow seat and the others placed for stress, with the last one well ahead of the stern paddler who may want to knee paddle. They are not meant to be seats!

The seats are set as low as possible for passenger balance and legroom in the canoe. Remember that the higher the weight position the less balance you will have in the canoe. For this reason, in stiff winds and rough waters it is better to knee paddle than sit up high in the canoe.

The rush cushions in more expensive canoes are more comfortable than the hard wood or metal seats, but the use of a small waterproof cushion can alleviate discomfort. Cover aluminum seats with rug material that can be removed if it gets wet, or simply bring along a small cushion for the fanny. Shallow canoes mean that the legs will be extended more laterally than in a canoe with more depth. Comfort, then, is determined by the depth of the canoe and the elevation of the seat in a given design.

Why the choice of 15-, 16-, 17-, and 18-foot lengths? As a general rule, it is a matter of use and the amount of weight to be carried. It is also a matter of design. The 18-foot canoe has been the standard of wilderness travel for generations since it will carry two people and a lot of duffle safely and with a good margin of height needed in rough water conditions. As you go down to the 17-footer you lose a bit of height; since its width is maintained within an inch or so, the canoe is generally a bit fatter. The 16 will be a good deal squattier as will the 15. Generally speaking, the longer canoe is more stable in a given design mode, but the length and weight might be excessive for its intended use. If the canoe is to be used only as a lakeside recreation vehicle, 18 feet is not really necessary unless there will be one or two passengers. There is no need for extra carrying capacity, so the 16 or even the 15 is recommended. We have recently gone from the 17 to the 15 for our use because the 15 is lighter, easier to load and carry, and easier to maneuver. I broke into canoeing, however, with an 18-foot guide model when I was a youngster, and it was a tough canoe to handle alone in a wind.

A prime factor in choosing length is the design of the hull and its relationship to the length. A basic design, improved little from Indian days, is the flat-bottomed curve design, which is meant to settle into the water with the greatest stability. This flat bottom is, of course, shallowed at the bow and stern so that the canoe does not act like a barge. The curve of the hull as seen from above is modified in many ways depending upon the designer (see fig. 5).

The flatter bottom design in a narrow shape is for speed and white water use. Its advantages are quicker response and equally stable performance. However, it generally has lower sides and less carry-

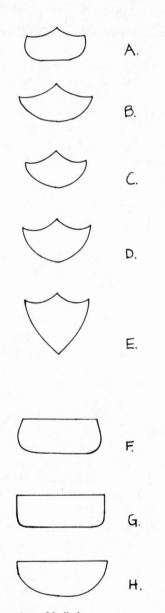

Figure 5. Cross section view of hull shapes.
(A) *Flat bottom.* (B) *Shallow arch.* (C) *Shallow vee.* (D) *Rounded vee.* (E) *Deep vee.*
(F) *Tumblehome.* (G) *Straight sides.* (H) *Flare.*

ing capacity. The tumblehome, with its inward curving on top, adds much to the hull strength. Many racing models do not have this or require it.

The "slower" canoes have a deeper keel; the racing models have a flat keel or no keel at all. The workhorse 20-footers usually have bilge keels in addition to a center "shoe" keel. These add stability and also help the canoe over rock river bottoms.

The more rounded design is a tippier canoe but has the advantage of more speed. The modified V-type hull is a very fast canoe but sacrifices balance and stability. It performs to the extreme.

You can see that canoe design generally is a matter of give and take. The deep-running steady workhorse canoe will not perform as well as the sleek racer. The middle ground between these two will often lack both requirements, though it will be a delight to handle unless you are an extremely sensitive canoeist used to instant reaction from your craft under stressful conditions.

The most common canoe for recreational use is the flat-bottomed model that is designed for general use, not top performance. It will respond to all conditions depending on the facility of the user. It is important that the user be aware of the capabilities in order to get the most in performance as with any boat, car, or horse. A neophyte in a sophisticated canoe will not usually perform as well as an expert in an old-style workhorse design.

Canoe weight is a major factor in selection. If it is imperative that you use a lightweight canoe because of frequent portaging or if you require a lighter canoe for loading and unloading, you can arrive at the proper weight by sacrificing length, strength, and type of construction. You'll have to treat it more gently, though. The lightest canoes are those that are built of wood planks and are not covered, even with fiberglass or canvas. The plastics used today for canoe hulls are generally heavier. Aluminum is the best weight compromise in relation to strength and ability to stand up under stress.

TYPES OF CANOES

Described here are the basic types for canoe design. Study this classification system in order to arrive at a perspective on the various designs, lengths, and uses as they relate to your requirements.

Casual recreation canoes are usually built of functional materials, and cost is a primary consideration. Quite often they are not of long-lasting material or the best construction, but they will certainly serve the casual canoeist for many years with careful use and proper storage, usually out in the backyard. Safety is a key feature of the design while high performance is not. You cannot have both despite what the catalogues say.

Day tripper/weekender canoes are designed to carry more weight though not excessive cargo. They will safely handle two canoeists with their weekend baggage up to about 600 pounds. The good ones are lightweight and therefore portable, fairly responsive on the water, and from 16 feet to 18 feet long.

Touring canoes are really the traveler's boat. They are generally long and slender and designed for medium volume capacity but with lower sides and a lower profile. Speed and ease in paddling are a must. They usually are flat with no traditional canoe peak.

Wilderness tripping canoes are built to carry a large amount of weight for extended trips into remote areas. They are high-sided and heavily built to withstand all kinds of rough conditions. Usually 18 feet or longer, they are optionally equipped for a motor. Some are square-sterned models specifically designed for motors.

Downriver canoes are designed for instant maneuverability under quick-changing current conditions and for paddling around obstructions. They are very good for fast paddling in a straight line. As medium volume carriers they will perform well except in fast white water conditions.

Competition cruising canoes are built to standard specifications for racing, up to 18½ feet. They are somewhat slower to maneuver since they are designed for straight-out speed. Not generally suitable for heavy in-depth cruising, they have very low profiles, and thus they are not suited for high wave conditions or curvy river traveling.

White water playboat canoes are very maneuverable, will carry high volume, are constructed for high stress, and are practically indestructible. They run to around 18 feet, though generally they are confined to 16 and 17 feet.

Solo canoes are traveling canoes for wilderness use and some racing. They feature exacting maneuverability and ease of portage. They are fast and under 16 feet. Usually from 12 to 15 feet is desirable. Solo sport and solo white water canoes are strictly a specialty.

The accompanying table compares seven brands in the day tripper/weekender category. These were selected from a listing in *Canoe* magazine *Buyer's Guide 1982*. The listing shows a small but typical sample of the variety of canoes available in this category. Look at the canoe shapes and designs in figures 6 and 7. Note, too, the hull shapes that have been developed for these specific requirements.

Comparison of Day Tripper/Weekender Canoes

Material[a]	Length (ft.)	Width (in.)	Depth (in.)	Hull[b]	Weight (lbs.)
RX	15½	34	14	C/SY/SV/F	65
FG	16¼	37	14½	W/SY/SA/T	90
PL	17	37	15	S/SY/SV/F	54
RX	17¼	36	15	W/SY/FB/T	78
AL	17—light-weight	36	13⅛	S/SY/FB/T	60
FG	16	36	12	SA	70
WO	16	35	12	W/S/SA/T	76

[a]Materials
  WO—wood
  AL—aluminum alloy
  FG—fiberglass chopper gun
    and matt
  PL—proprietary layup
    (specific mfg. specs)
  RX—Royalex
    (vinyl—ABS—foam
    sandwich)

[b]Canoe shapes
  S—straight sides
  W—straight with rise at ends
  C—moderately rockered or curved
  SY—symmetrical
  FB—flat bottom
  SA—shallow arch
  SV—shallow V
  T—tumblehome
  F—flare

CANOE MATERIALS

There are many materials for canoes, as well as combinations of materials. Fiberglass and resin compounds and newer materials are constantly coming on the market (see table).

Wood is the first and primary material. Usually, there is cedar planking on ash or oak ribs, or in some cases no ribs at all. Oak trim is also used on some canoes. The conventional "old style" canoe of the past is the wood canoe with a canvas skin. A variation is the wood canoe with clear glass outside and inside for additional strength and crash protection.

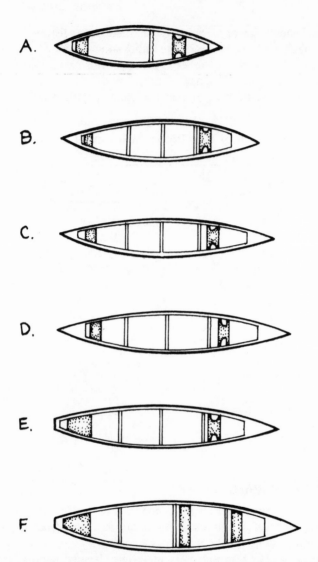

Figure 6.   Several canoe shapes (viewed from above) of standard-type canoes show-ing the relationship of form to length. Note that the shorter the canoe the wider in relationship to length. The shorter the canoe in this perspective of relationship of length to width, the less maneuverable it will be. (A) The 13 foot with straight keel. (B) The 15 foot, also with straight keel. (C) The 17 foot with a slight rise at both ends, actually the 15 footer but with raised ends. (D) The 18 footer with raised ends. (E and F) The square stern models in 17 and 19 foot lengths (Grumman).

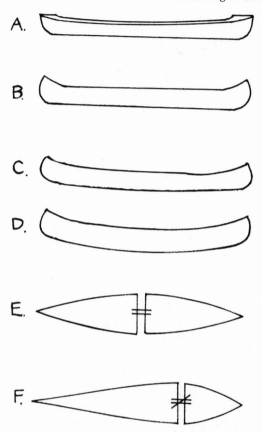

Figure 7. Viewed from the side are various forms of canoe design. (A) Straight flat keel to the curve. (B) Straight with raised keel at both ends. (C) Moderately rockered. (D) Extremely rockered. (E) Symmetrical. (F) Asymmetrical. Reasons for these differences are many and you will learn about them from experience as you progress.

From years of observation and use experts report that aluminum is still the best material for canoes. The liveries certainly bear out this point since most of them rent aluminum canoes exclusively. The aluminum canoe manufacturers give more inclusive guarantees for their craft than manufacturers for synthetics do. Aluminum canoes also seem to hold up better on the secondhand market. The aluminum canoe manufacturers, however, have not progressed as much in meeting the critical demands made by the super experts for more sensuous canoe designs. In time they may, but for the present the three biggest aluminum canoe makers seem content with standard middle-of-the-road designs which most people prefer.

Aluminum is noisy and gets cold and hot, but there are ways to overcome these problems. To cut down the noise of an aluminum canoe, you can buy plastic rubber strips and attach them to the gunwales to avoid paddle bang. We use green indoor-outdoor carpet sections fore and aft and in the middle, and we also wrap the thwarts with the same material.

All of the most exciting new canoe shapes and designs are made with fiberglass. Most are slimmer, with lower freeboard and more speed as a result. They are somewhat easier to control in a wind because they have no risers at the ends.

But it is easy in this day of discount prices to get workmanship of inferior quality for that very low price. Stay away from canoes made of cheap materials. The weakest material is chopper matting often found in budget canoes. If you see one like this, it is okay if it has the cloth weave behind it on the inside of the canoe. It is not the best by any means, but it is adequate for simple use as long as the canoe is not strained or run into snags and rocks and the like.

A step above chopper matting is glass cloth in various thicknesses and mesh sizes. The strongest reinforcement is called glass roving, somewhat like an actual woven cloth.

Many of the better glass canoes are made from Royalex and Kevlar. These modern plastics have distinctive qualities of strength, stiffness, ability to be molded into unlimited shapes, durability, and puncture resistance.

5

Cartop Carriers

There is a host of cartop carriers designed to carry everything from lumber, surfboards, bicycles, and boxes to kayaks, boats, and canoes. Most of them are simple in design and built to varying degrees of efficiency, durability, and strength. The conventional cartop carrier with two bars that extend across the car roof is the most versatile and most popular. It can be equipped with a roll bar for loading the canoe from the back of the car, thus avoiding lifting the canoe straight from the side and then dropping it down on the cross bars (see figs. 8 and 9).

A simpler design involves four styrofoam blocks, formed flat to fit the car roof and grooved to fit into the canoe gunwales. When they are placed evenly across the roof, the canoe sits firmly in them. It is tied down at bow and stern and hooked into the rain gutters of the car with two cross ties or hooked into the car doors for extra safety. The tying straps are either of solid rubber that stretches or nylon that ties down tight (see fig. 9). This rig sets the canoe lower on the car, offering less chance for wind to get under the craft and lift it up, but it is not considered as safe against sudden stops or

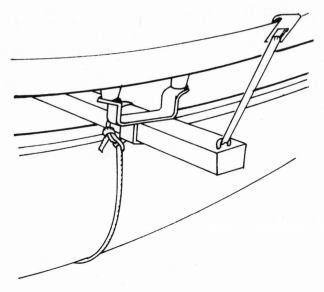

Figure 8. Typical cartop carrier with crossbar and strong grips to hold to the car rain gutter or door. Tiedowns are bow and stern with two straps across and over the canoe attached to the car.

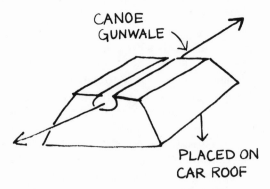

CANOE
GUNWALE

PLACED ON
CAR ROOF

Figure 9. Typical styrofoam block and rubber strip grips used with bow and stern tiedown.

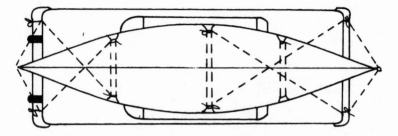

Figure 10. Emergency cross tying if no cartop rig is available.

starts as the conventional rack. Beware of cheap racks, though, or ones that will rust out quickly or not support the canoe securely.

Many canoeists stick to the very simple methods. They may mount their canoe on four pillows on the roof and tie it down with two ties across and at bow and stern. This method is not recommended.

6

Paddles

Place any beginner in a canoe, hand him any paddle, and he'll manage to pull his weight. He will not know that there are infinite varieties of paddles that could help him in many ways to increase his efficiency on the water. Over the years the expert will have tried out and owned several paddle designs and will have settled on one or two paddles that he uses under varied conditions. The racer will use one type of paddle, the cruiser another, and the casual canoer another.

The Indians designed quite narrow canoe paddle blades. Perhaps this was necessary because they were working with narrow pieces of wood. To this day those narrow paddles are used widely under all sorts of conditions; canoeists have been paddling with them for many years and these paddles have become an extension of the arm.

This is not to say that we have not come up with better ideas and designs for paddles to be used under specific conditions. Whether it is profitable to own three sets of canoe paddles for the three basic types of waters is a moot point. Some canoeists do. As you begin to develop your paddling style and become more expert at it, perhaps

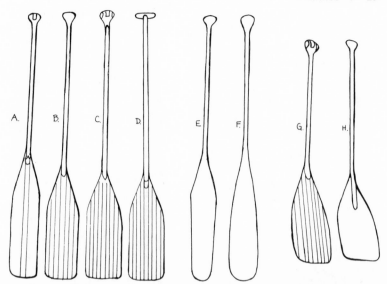

Figure 11. Paddle types. (A) River. (B) Voyager. (C) Sugar Island. (D) T grip. (E) Ottertail. (F) Beavertail. (G) Bent touring. (H) Marathon. (Labels from Grey Owl Paddle Co.) These are typical designs followed by the industry. Some are made from only one piece of wood; others are laminated from several kinds of wood including even balsa in some cases for extremely light handling.

you will decide to use several paddles — a narrow one for easy paddling, a wider blade for upstream or waters that require more subtle motions, and still another for racing and traveling long distances over open water.

Old-timers are slow to change. Take the present-day wide-blade paddles for example. They are not the slim, graceful paddles of yesteryear; they look like clubs. But place one in the water on stroke and you can instantly see that it offers you almost twice the efficiency of the slimmer design. The old-timer argues that a bigger paddle moves more water, but it takes more energy to do it. If you are used to the pace of a narrow paddle, it is hard to adjust to the wide blade, even though it would really take less energy to do so. The modern canoeist used to the wide blade would have an equally difficult time adjusting to the narrow version.

Judging from the canoe liveries, the wide-blade paddle is the most acceptable. It doesn't break unless you run over it with a car, and

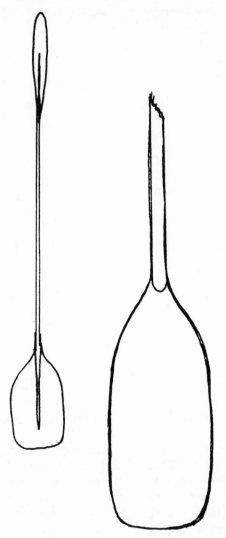

Figure 12.   Paddle types (continued). Double paddle feathered to 90 degrees.

the plastic blade seems to hold up under duress. It is light, well balanced, and does the job for most people. If the fact that these paddles are not fashioned from fine woods in classical shapes doesn't bother you, you will find them acceptable.

So the choice of the proper canoe paddle is one to deal with from day one, the time you begin to set your paddling pace in relation to requirements of speed and maneuverability. Stick to your choice and adapt to it in terms of stroke pace and the subtleties of paddling. Changing paddles too often will destroy the set movements of arms and body and cause undue fatigue.

In addition to various blade styles, there is a variety of paddle handle designs ranging from the old-fashioned pear-shaped end grip to the more modern T grip. Again, there is a choice to be made.

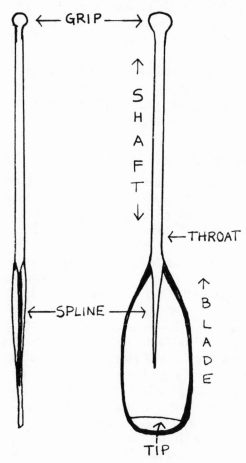

Figure 13. Paddle nomenclature.

Changing from one to the other can be bothersome, yet I know some paddlers that do just that to avoid strain on their hands and wrists. On a long trip they carry both styles.

Originally, paddles were handmade exclusively of wood. Some handwork was needed even when automatic machines turned out paddles from raw lumber—just like baseball bats. This, of course, became costly. There are several nationally known paddle manufacturers who make their paddles of laminated woods of different species. Their paddles are as beautifully made as a piece of expensive furniture. While these paddles do not have the strength of aluminum and plastic, they are a delight to handle. Just don't use a wooden paddle to fend off rocks, dig holes, kill rattlesnakes, or hack at tent poles.

Think of your canoe paddle as you would your golf club, hunting bow, or baseball bat. Not just any one will do. In the long run, a quality paddle fit to your measurements and paddling style will be worth what you will have to pay for it.

BENT PADDLES

The latest design in paddles is the bent paddle. It has had some difficulty in becoming broadly accepted, except by racers and open water sprinters. The bent paddle is the answer to a dream, and once you have tried it you will discard the old stick for all but the shortest trip.

The reason the bent paddle was not invented earlier is that no one could make it until the process of lamination was developed. Bent paddles are made exclusively from laminates, though the plastic developers will likely come up with plastic-molded bent designs in the near future. Even aluminum is now used in the bent paddle.

Why the bent paddle? Well, look at the paddles in motion and you will see that for the same physical exertion you gain about 20 percent more sweep in the water if you use a bent paddle. That is quite an advantage, especially if you are racing or paddling under trying water conditions where instant power is needed to avoid a rock, swing in a current, or fight waves. Bent paddles cost more, generally, but are well worth the price.

Beware of cheap wood paddles, or even cheap laminated wood paddles. Quite often they are made without much care and with

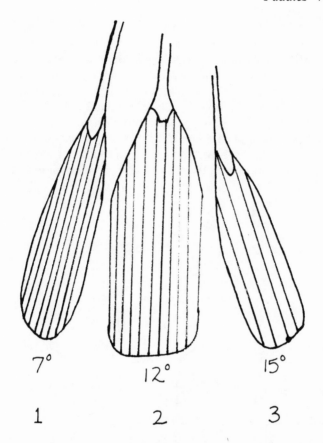

Figure 14.   Several typical bent paddle designs, ranging from 7-degree pitch to 15 degrees (angle of bend). The 15s are mostly for racing.

woods that are unsuitable or insufficiently aged. They look nice, but, as usual, you pay for what you get in this line. While it seems a bit odd to have to pay a good price for a well-made paddle, consider that in 1928 when I ordered my first Old Town 18-foot guide-model canoe, it cost $75 delivered. That same canoe today costs nearly $2,000. So the price of a canoe paddle has rightly gone up, and if you pay over $50 for a good wooden one, that is certainly not out of line.

PADDLE FIT

Yes, the proper length paddle is a must if you are to enjoy your times afloat and render your energy in the most economical way. Paddles are made in standard lengths from 4 feet to 6 feet.

There is a simple rule of thumb for choosing a paddle for flat water touring. Sit on the canoe seat and place the paddle blade in the water to the depth usually used in paddling, just where the top of the blade reaches the water surface (see fig. 15). The grip should then be at your shoulder height. Now, with the grip at shoulder level, the upper arm should be horizontal, the most efficient position for general pad-

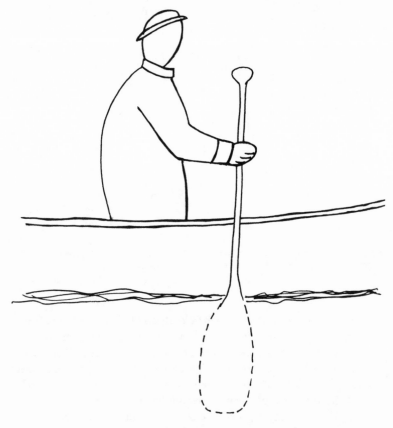

Figure 15. Paddler holding paddle in proper position for measuring fit.

dling—a bit higher for extra paddling power without having to reach too far forward with the body in an awkward position.

Most adults will select a 54-inch paddle. When you are sitting, the distance from your seat to your shoulder, not your overall height, is relevant to paddle size. Whether you are a tall or a short person, your body trunk size will be about the same. The old rule of shorter paddle for the stern is not necessarily true, even though it is necessary for the bow paddler to be able to reach over the wider part of the canoe in order to place his paddle into the water properly and follow through with the total stroke.

If you have stern paddled and have found that you have to bend forward or down in order to dig the paddle in properly, the paddle is too short for you except in very mild and easy work. Get a paddle an inch or two longer. To prove the point use the longer bow paddle for a few strokes. Though it might be too long, it will be better than one that is too short. For more power and deeper submersion into the water—as in white water canoeing—a longer paddle is proper and still can be used for casual paddling with minimal fatigue.

7

Canoe Care and Repair

The best way to keep from having to repair a canoe is to paddle it safely around obstructions and refrain from crashing into the dock, a rock, or hard place. But even the best of intentions is overruled by the law of accident. You may hit or scrape something creating a damaging hole in the canoe shell. If you are lucky enough to get to shore before everything aboard is soaked, you have to set to work immediately repairing the damage, at least well enough to get you to civilization and perhaps some professional help. What to do in the meantime?

Inspect one hundred canoes afloat even on long trips and you probably will not find one with a repair kit aboard. If they do have one, the canoeists will be found wanting in actual experience. They are like people who carry spare tires in the back of their cars and seldom check them for air or know how to change a tire.

Yes, damage can happen, and when it does you had better be prepared. You are not alone. Any boat owner is up against the same odds. There might not be any repair shops along your lake or waterway, especially if you are on a run between highways with no signs of civilization.

Carry a repair kit with you. There are kits available for all materials from which canoes are made. Yes, there are even aluminum repair kits, although fiberglass will do a temporary job to keep you afloat. Learn how to use the kit, what proportions of plastics to mix, and how to apply them.

Learn all about your canoe and its manufacture and have available all the necessary materials and equipment for dealing with the wound. The repair kit in the boat is as important as the snakebite kit and the first aid kit. Know how to use it, especially if you are going on a long jaunt and expect never to see another living person along the route. We do not know a single canoeist who knows how to mix and apply resins and the like. Most of them can't fix a dent in their own cars.

In the absence of a repair kit, is there any other way to repair the tear, break, or puncture temporarily? You had better know some way to do it or you will have to leave your entire rig behind and make a long and arduous walk back to the road. We would rather scare you now as you read this in the comfort of your home rather than have you blame us for not warning you.

Recently we were able to repair a bad tear by applying duct tape wrapped over the hole in overlapping strips. It kept the water out but was pretty soggy by the time we got back to base. A passing boater answered our hail for help, and luckily he had aboard his

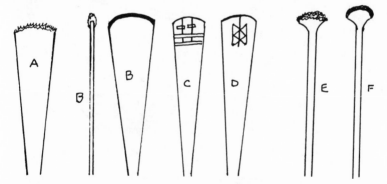

Figure 16. A sample of paddle repair. (A) Roughed edges. Sand down, dry completely, and refinish. (B) Split. Splice temporarily across both sides with duct tape. Reglue later and reinforce with copper wire sewed into the wood and refinish. Grip rough? Sand down, dry thoroughly, shellac, and sand down. Fill with plastic wood for even contour.

boat a roll of the duct tape which he had meant to return to his home workshop.

Other care precautions you should take include cleaning out the canoe with a brush and a water hose and wiping slime and other muck from the outside of the canoe. You never can tell what you are riding through. Oil is particularly destructive to fiberglass and to some resins. Acid rain is no help either. If you do get a dent in the canoe, push the dent back or pound it out so that the canoe bottom is smooth and water-resistant. Inspect the bottom for even small cracks or cuts each time before you go out, and make the necessary repairs. Check the thwart and end cap screws for tightness and make sure all are secure. Inspect and replace bow and stern lines; a rotted line will not hold if you have to be towed home. The same goes for the ropes if you use them for your cartop tiedowns.

Store your canoe out of the elements, particularly if it is made of glass or any of the plastics. The moment a plastic canoe is exposed to the weather it slowly begins to decompose — just like nylon fishing line or rope. As aircraft manufacturers discovered, only aluminum will bear up under all weather conditions. This is the reason they use it in their planes.

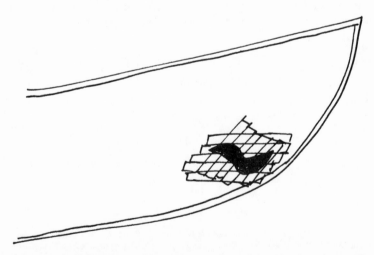

Figure 17. A sample of our crisis repair using duct tape on aluminum canoe. The same can be done on any other canoe material as a temporary patch. Patch both inside and out.

If your canoe is of wooden structure, store it in a dry place away from heat or excessive cold and certainly out of the sun. The greatest enemy to wood is dry rot, and damp rot can penetrate even a good paint job on a canvas-covered canoe. Don't expect even the toughest glass over wood to be impervious to weather.

Check your paddles occasionally for dents, breaks, and weak points. In general, keep your eyes open at all times for problems, and solve them before they become monsters. Especially if your paddles are costly and made of wood, treat them as you would an expensive fly rod, a set of golf clubs, or a camera. Keep them under cover. Don't leave them to bake in the sun or to become saturated in the rain even if they are painted with so-called miracle finishes. If the ends become burred from constant rubbing on rocks and gravel, shave them off, dry them thoroughly, and refinish them before the breaks or rot sets in for certain. To store the paddles, lay them flat on two bars or on a shelf. Don't stack them against the wall or they will take a "set." If a bent paddle is damaged this way, it is an abomination.

8

Canoeing with a Motor

Paddling a long lake against the wind can be a tiring proposition. Paddling upstream against a current of over two miles an hour can also be taxing. If you face these types of conditions, the use of a motor can aid greatly in outdoor enjoyment. The motor is also used quite effectively in trolling a lake or river.

Using a motor on a canoe less than 16 feet in length is not recommended. Unless the motor is extremely light, like some of the electric trolling motors generally used on small fishing skiffs and prams, it is a very tippy proposition. No canoe is rated to carry a motor over five horsepower, and, except for straight-out driving over glassy water, the speed should be kept low. The slightest wave can tip a moving canoe very quickly, and body movement doesn't always correct the situation in time.

The motorized canoe is really very unorthodox. Basically the canoe is not designed for this kind of power. If you require motorized travel over open water, you would be better off in a wide skiff or pram and be done with the canoe except for waters where those boats cannot go. Oh, yes, the natives of Newfoundland travel the rivers in

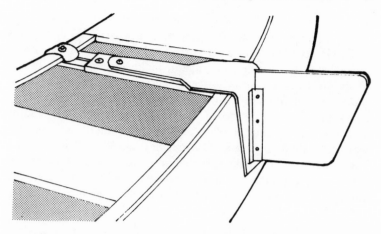

Figure 18. Typical outboard motor bracket (Grumman) located behind the rear canoe seat for motor on the left side.

24-foot-long wooden canoes that are square sterned and designed to carry motors of ten and even fifteen horsepower to get them through rapids and rock-strewn eddies. They wear out a couple of propellers in a season up there guiding fishermen and hunters. We have seen times when the boat was actually pushed through sand and gravel by a propeller digging into the bottom because the water was so shallow. But this kind of use is not for everybody.

The canoe motor can be attached to an ordinary double-ended canoe by the use of a simple bracket attached behind the stern seat to both gunwales. The double-ended canoe has a nearly vertical pad for attaching the motor which is mounted on the left side of the canoe, preferably. (see fig. 18). The shaft is designed for shallow driving with the prop barely beneath the water surface. This depth can be changed by the canoeist moving forward in the canoe to raise the stern end a little or leaning back to sink the propeller down a little into the water. In some cases when traveling through shallows the canoeists both move as far forward as possible, barely allowing the propeller to be submerged. Plastic propellers are now available and are very practical for stream and shallow water running.

The motorized canoe is tricky to handle. Don't make any sudden turns or leave your hands off the steering mechanism for a moment.

If, for some reason, the prop hits an underground snag and turns the motor abruptly, you can easily be tipped over. While it looks great to be speeding along a glassy river or lake, make sure you maintain balance at all times, and again, make your turns easily and slowly. In order not to hit unseen snags or rocks and damage the canoe, proceed slowly unless you can see plainly into the water. When approaching land, slow down to a stop well before your landing approach and use your paddle. A sudden stop can throw you overboard or give everything aboard a shuffling that is really unnecessary.

Before taking off, make sure that your engine bracket is secured to the canoe and that the motor is secured to the bracket. Check your fuel supply and remember to bring it from the car to the canoe.

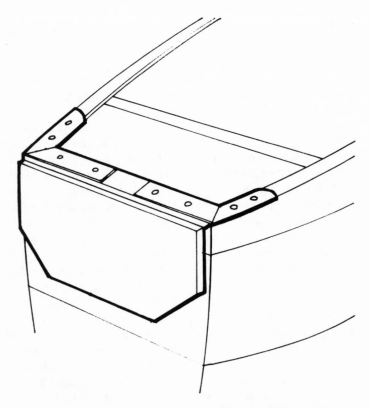

Figure 19. Square stern canoe and motor panel (Grumman).

Remember that canoes other than the strict wooden types have styrofoam inserts bow and stern for flotation. Since oil and gas will disintegrate this material very quickly, watch the spills and inspect the flotation once in a while to make sure it is still there.

For very weak power in comparison to the 5 hp outboard motor generally used, you can select an electric trolling motor used by fishermen to propel their boats. This is a quiet motor and operates on batteries rather than smelly fuel. While it does not offer the power of the bigger gasoline motor, it just might offer enough for ordinary needs. It is much lighter and less bulky and can easily be portaged if this becomes necessary.

To be legal on all waterways, a permit and serial number on your canoe is needed when you use a motor. It must be renewed annually.

SQUARE STERN CANOES

The 18-foot and longer models include the square stern canoe which is generally used with a motor. The stern plate is mounted with a slab of wood so that the turn knobs penetrate the wood to keep the motor from moving and slipping (see fig. 19). It should be checked regularly since the motor may receive bumps that can go unnoticed until it just flips off and you hear a sizzle behind you as the motor goes under.

The square stern model sometimes comes with a spray rail along both sides of the canoe for wave deflection. Some models are even molded with a kind of bulge to aid in wave deflection.

Don't buy a square stern canoe unless you intend to use the motor most of the time. When paddled, the square stern drags in the current unmercifully, holding you back and restricting maneuverability.

9

Accessories for Safety and Comfort

FLOTATION DEVICES

Canoeing is a very simple sport requiring a minimum of equipment beyond the paddles. Legal requirements include either U.S. Coast Guard–approved life jackets or lifesaving cushions for everyone aboard. Most canoeists choose the cushions because they make good seat cushions and are soft and useful to sit on when ashore. Cameras and other equipment such as binoculars can be rested on them when not in use.

The cushion should not be attached to the seat or thwarts, however, because in an emergency it must be instantly available to throw overboard if needed to help a person in the water. When used for lifesaving, it is mounted on the person so that he rides in the water in an upright position. This means putting the arms through the loops so that the cushion rides on the chest (see fig. 20).

For white water canoeing, on a windy, rough lake, or in ocean surf, the life vest should be worn at all times. Yes, even the best of swimmers have been known to drown. Nonswimmers should wear vests at all times when questionable water is encountered. This is up to the captain (stern paddler) to enforce.

Personal Flotation Devices

Coast Guard regulations in Part 175 of Title 33, Code of Federal Regulations, require personal flotation devices in the following three situations:

(1) No person may use a recreational boat less than 16 feet in length or a canoe or kayak unless at least one personal flotation device (PFD) of the following types is on board for each person:
(a) Type I PFD
(b) Type II PFD
(c) Type III PFD
(d) Type IV PFD

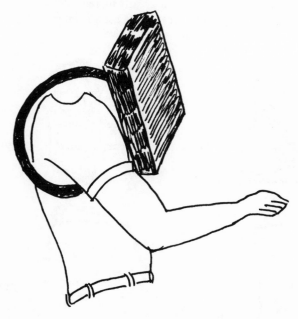

Figure 20. Correct method of wearing a life preserver cushion. Mount the cushion on the chest and lie forward on it to keep the face out of the water. Don't mount it on your back since your face would be in the water.

(2) No person may use a recreational boat 16 feet or more in length, except a canoe or kayak, unless at least one personal flotation device of the following types is on board for each person:
  (a) Type I PFD
  (b) Type II PFD
  (c) Type III PFD
(3) No person may use a recreational boat 16 feet or more in length, except a canoe or kayak, unless one Type IV PFD is on board in addition to the PFDs required in paragraph (1).

There are five types of personal flotation devices. (Note: These are designed to perform as described in calm water and when the wearer is not wearing any other flotation material, such as a wetsuit.)

A Type I PFD has the greatest required buoyancy and is designed to turn most unconscious persons in the water from a face down position to a vertical and slightly backward position. By maintaining the person in that position, it greatly increases his or her chances of survival. The Type I PFD is suitable for all waters, especially for

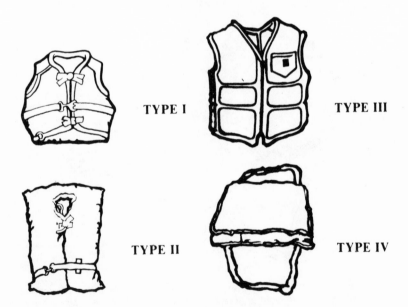

TYPE I   TYPE III

TYPE II   TYPE IV

Figure 21.   Personal flotation devices.

cruising on waters where there is a probability of delayed rescue, such as large bodies of water where it is not likely that a significant number of boats will be in close proximity. This type of PFD is the most effective of all the types in rough water. The Type I PFD is easiest to don in any emergency because it is reversible and available in only two sizes — adult (90 lbs. or more) and child (less than 90 lbs.) — which are designed to fit all persons in the appropriate category.

A Type II PFD is designed to turn the wearer to a vertical and slightly backward position in the water. The turning action is not as pronounced as with a Type I, and the device will not turn as many persons under the same conditions as the Type I. The Type II PFD is usually more comfortable to wear than the Type I. This type PFD is normally sized for ease of emergency donning and is available in the following sizes: adult (more than 90 lb.), medium child (50 lb. to 90 lb.), and two categories of small child (less than 50 lb. or less than 30 lb.). Additionally, some models are sized by chest sizes. You may prefer to use the Type II where there is a probability of quick rescue, such as areas where it is common for other persons to be engaged in boating, fishing, and other water activities.

The Type III PFD is designed so that the wearer can place himself or herself in a vertical and slightly backward position. It will maintain the wearer in that position and have no tendency to turn him face down. A Type III can be the most comfortable, comes in a variety of styles which should be matched to the individual use, and is usually the best choice for water sports, such as skiing, hunting, fishing, canoeing, and kayaking. This type of PFD normally comes in many chest sizes and weight ranges; however, some universal sizes are available. You may also prefer to use the Type III where there is a probability of quick rescue.

A Type IV PFD is designed to be grasped and held by the user until he is rescued, as well as to be thrown to a person who has fallen overboard. While the Type IV is acceptable in place of a wearable device in certain instances, this type is suitable only where there is a probability of quick rescue. It is not recommended for nonswimmers and children.

A Type V PFD is approved for restricted uses. No Type V PFD is currently approved for use on recreational boats to meet the mandatory carriage requirements of the Coast Guard.

You are required by Federal Regulations to have at least one Coast Guard-approved personal flotation device for each person in your recreational boat. You may not use your recreational boat unless all your PFDs are in serviceable condition, are readily accessible, are legibly marked with the Coast Guard approval number, and are of an appropriate size (within the weight range and chest sizes marked on the PFD) for each person on board.

Your PFD provides buoyancy to help keep your head above the water and to help you remain in a satisfactory position in the water. The average weight of an adult is only ten to twelve pounds in the water, and the buoyancy provided by the PFD will support that weight in water. Unfortunately, your body weight does not determine how much you will weigh in water. In fact, your weight in water changes slightly throughout the day. There is no simple method of determining your weight in water. You should try the device in the water to make sure it supports your mouth out of the water. Remember, all straps, zippers, and tie tapes must be used, and of course the PFD must be the proper size (size limitations are on the label).

USCG approval of the PFD does not imply that it is ideal for all uses. For instance, there are a number of PFDs which are better suited for water skiing and others for white water canoeing and kayaking. These and other PFDs are labeled accordingly. Some PFDs are more rugged and durable than others but usually cost more. You should evaluate the trade-offs of cost, your intended use, and how often the PFD will have to be replaced. The use of most Type IV throwable PFDs usually requires you to grasp the device until rescued, which could prove difficult if there is an extended delay or if you are overcome by hypothermia (loss of body heat to the water). Also, USCG approval implies that if you find yourself in the water there will be someone available to throw a PFD to you.

For your PFD to function properly, follow these suggestions to insure that it fits, floats, and remains in good condition:

(1) Try your wearable PFD on and adjust it until it fits comfortably in and out of the water.

(2) Try your PFD out in the water. This will show you how it works and will give you confidence when you use it. You should be aware that your PFD may perform differently

under various conditions, such as in swift water or with bulky clothing.

(3) Mark your PFD with your name if you are the only wearer.

(4) Do not alter your PFD. If it does not fit properly, get one that does. An altered device is no longer Coast Guard approved.

(5) Your PFD is not intended for use as a fender or kneeling pad.

(6) Inspect your PFD periodically to ensure that it is free of rips, tears, or holes, that the flotation pads have no leaks, and that all seams and joints are securely sewn.

(7) Keep your PFD away from sharp objects which may rip the fabric or puncture the flotation pads.

(8) If your PFD contains kapok, the kapok fibers may become waterlogged and lose their buoyancy after the vinyl inserts are split or punctured. When the kapok becomes hard or if the kapok is soaked with water, the PFD is no longer serviceable. It may not work when you need it and must be replaced.

(9) If your PFD is wet, allow it to dry thoroughly before storing it. Store it in a well-ventilated area.

(10) Do not dry your PFD in front of a radiator or other source of direct heat.

(11) If you must swim while wearing your PFD use a back or side stroke.

It is difficult for a child to float in a safe position because of the distribution of body weight and because a child tends to panic when suddenly in an unfamiliar environment. The violent movement of the arms and legs in an attempt to "climb out" of the water tends to nullify the stability of the PFD. An approved device will keep a child afloat but not always in a face up position. A child should be taught how to put on the device and should be allowed to try it out in the water. It is important that the child feels comfortable and knows what the PFD is for and how it functions. Parents should note, however, that PFDs are not a substitute for adult supervision.

Your personal flotation device will not help you if you don't have it on. If you don't choose to wear it at all times, you should keep it handy and put it on when severe weather threatens or when danger is imminent. Don't wait until it is too late; nonswimmers and children especially should wear their PFDs at all times when on or near the water.

Hypothermia is a major cause of death in boating accidents. Often the cause of death is listed as drowning; but, most often the primary cause is hypothermia and the secondary cause is drowning. After an individual has succumbed to hypothermia, he will lose consciousness and then drown. The accompanying chart shows the effects of hypothermia.

PFDs can increase survival time because of the insulation they provide. Naturally, the warmer the water, the less insulation one will require. When operating in cold water (below 40° F.) consideration should be given to using a coat- or jacket-style PFD as they cover more of the body than the vest-style PFDs.

Effects of Hypothermia

Water Temperature (°F.)	Exhaustion Unconsciousness	Expected Time of Survival
32.5	Under 15 min.	Under 15 to 45 min.
32.5 to 40	15 to 30 min.	30 to 90 min.
40 to 50	30 to 60 min.	1 to 3 hrs.
50 to 60	1 to 2 hrs.	1 to 6 hrs.
60 to 70	2 to 7 hrs.	2 to 40 hrs.
70 to 80	3 to 12 hrs.	3 hrs. to indefinite
Over 80	Indefinite	Indefinite

Some points to remember about hypothermia protection are:

(1) While afloat in the water, do not attempt to swim unless it is to reach a nearby craft, fellow survivor, or a floating object on which you can lean or climb. Unnecessary swimming increases the rate of body heat loss. In cold water, drownproofing methods that require putting your head in water are not recommended. Keep your head out of the water. This will greatly lessen heat loss and increase your survival time.

(2) Keep a positive attitude about your survival and rescue. This will improve your chances of extending your survival time until rescue. Your will-to-live does make a difference!

(3) If there is more than one person in the water, huddling is recommended while waiting to be rescued. This action tends to reduce the rate of heat loss and thus increases the survival time.

(4) Always wear your PFD. It won't help you fight off the effects of hypothermia if you don't have it on when you go into the water.

If you need more information about PFDs and safe recreational boating, contact your state boating authority, U.S. Coast Guard Auxiliary, U.S. Power Squadron, Red Cross, or your nearest unit of the U.S. Coast Guard.

FIRST AID KIT

Another safety device, although one that is not required by law, is the first aid kit. When needed, include a snakebite kit. You can make up your own kit including aspirin, medicine for bites and cuts, bandages, smelling salts, suntan lotion, hand lotion, scissors, razor blades, and any other drugstore items that might be needed for a day's run or an overnight or extended trip. This usually makes up into a small package that can be carried in a plastic bag and conveniently hung below the canoe seat (see fig. 22). Straps or some cord wrapped around the seat with enough room for the package will hold it tight enough, and it will be readily available when needed.

BAILER

A bailer is an absolute necessity even if the canoe is not swamped. A hard rain can add inches of water aboard and soak everything. Even an inch of water in a canoe can cause it to be very tippy. Attach the bailer to a thwart or to the seat — use one at each end — as standard equipment.

COMPASS

If you are canoeing in strange waters where definite shoreline identification is difficult, bring along a compass and use it for ori-

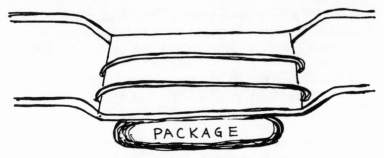

Figure 22. Method of securing a plastic package under the canoe seat. Use simple string or two straps, or make a baglike platform with strings at each end.

entation. In flat lands where you are cruising through a myriad of canals and cuts, all the surroundings may look alike, and it is quite easy to become confused about the way ahead or the way back. While you might not become permanently lost, a compass may help since it might take a good while to work your way out of the maze.

MAPS

A county map or several basic maps of the territory are most useful to study at home and bring along if you are on an extended trip. A geodetic map is the best for it shows the terrain of the area just in case you have to travel back to base on foot. Keep maps wrapped securely in a plastic bag and store with the first aid kits under the seats.

FOOD AND DRINK

Items for onboard comfort include thermos bottles filled with your favorite liquids such as pure water, coffee, and fruit juices and with good thick soup for cold-weather semi-meals. (Do not rely on natural water unless you boil it for 30 minutes.) We usually travel with his and hers coffee thermoses and two larger thermoses filled with either soup or juices such as V8 or orange juice. Even on a daylong trip, we also have a cooler that contains sandwiches, cookies, apples or oranges, and various goodies. We always stock plenty of food, for it is better to have too much than too little.

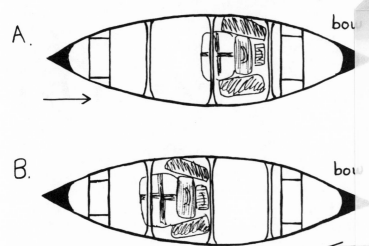

Figure 23.   Load the gear so that the bow is lower for going downstream (A *and*
higher for going upstream (B).

So far the list contains only very light items. Cooking and ca
ing equipment can mean a long list of items that have nothin
do with canoeing as such. The cookware and camping gear duf
should be carried in waterproof containers and stowed in the cen
of the canoe as low as possible so that the canoe balance is r
altered. Load the gear so that the bow is higher for going upstrea...
and lower when going downstream. It travels better this way.

ROPE AND TARP

Two fifty-foot coils of rope should be hung at bow and stern for
any number of reasons, including lining the canoe around falls and
rapids that you cannot paddle through. Under normal conditions
you will need rope for the anchor and canoe tie lines in addition
to any extra you will require for tiedowns for a shelter tarp used
for foul weather. For wet-weather canoeing a tarp which covers the
entire canoe is available. It has holes for the paddlers and is great
to have along to keep everything dry. Learn the knots in figure 24
for your safety and convenience.

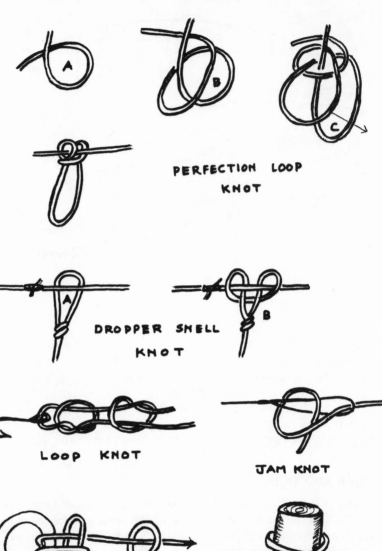

PERFECTION LOOP KNOT

DROPPER SNELL KNOT

LOOP KNOT

JAM KNOT

FISHERMAN'S BEND

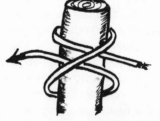

DOCK POLE HALF HITCH

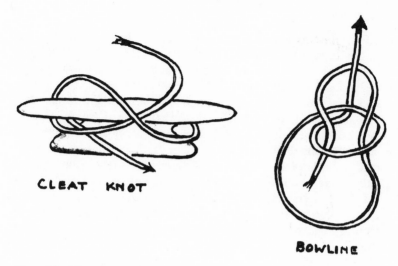

CLEAT KNOT

BOWLINE

Figure 24. These knots are very useful to boaters. Learn to tie them so well that you can tie them in the dark.

YOKE

If you plan to portage on the trip, you should have a yoke for shoulder comfort and ease of portage. There are several kinds on the market, each claiming to be the best. We recommend that you try out the various types in the store and decide on the one that you like best. Do the same for knee pads, in case you need something more than a cushion for knee paddling.

ANCHOR

A good anchor is a must for mooring the canoe off shore and also for dragging in a stiff wind or current where you want to proceed downstream at a slower pace than is dictated by the force of the current. We use a round ball or, failing that, a roundish rock which will not catch on sunken tree limbs or rocks and which can be discarded if it does become tangled. (It is no easy job to pull the canoe back upstream by the rope line and try to disentangle the anchor while the current is flipping you about mercilessly. Better to cut the rope and go look for another rock or anchor.)

FOOTWEAR

Since it is possible that you will be making landings where it will be unwise to drag the canoe up out of the water sufficiently for the crew to disembark, you are faced with alternatives in footwear. You can choose to land barefoot and wade ashore, thereby keeping your socks and shoes dry, or you can step overboard and get wet and then pull the canoe up on the sand or grassy bank. North country woodsmen usually wear leather-top, rubber-bottom boots that fill the bill adequately, but in warmer weather and southern climes, these boots tend to become too hot for traveling comfort. If you have an old pair of boots which you are ready to discard, you can cut the tops off them and merely slip off your shoes and slip on rubber boots. Do not sacrifice the canoe by dragging or pushing it up at an angle from the water. Better to get out while the canoe is still afloat and then drag or carry it up to dry land.

PASSENGER SEATS

A good, sturdy, comfortable seat is required for the passenger who is going to ride in the center of the canoe. Place the passenger just ahead of the forward thwart, not in front of the second thwart, since he would then be sitting too close to the stern paddler and would make it difficult for him to change paddle positions. Also, the balance is better with the passenger slightly ahead of the center of the canoe.

You can buy costly wood and rush collapsible seats that rest on the bottom of the canoe, or you can pick up an inexpensive "stadium seat" available at the drugstore or a variety store.

Many people find the low-style, aluminum-frame deck chairs quite comfortable, the only objection being that the passenger's weight is too high in the canoe. They are okay for easy waters and calm conditions, but they are not recommended for rough water, especially if the passenger is heavy.

Years ago, when a gentleman took his well-dressed lady out in the canoe for an afternoon paddle, the lady sat in an elaborately built slanted chair complete with cushions. This type of chair was comfortable but it is rarely seen today. You can make one from the sketch in figure 25 using light woods and brass screws and hinges.

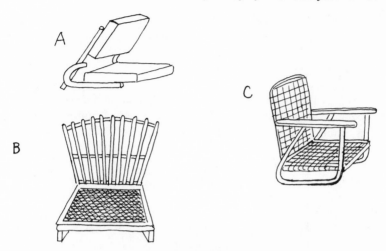

Figure 25. (A) *Collapsible passenger seat (stadium seat) set in front of thwart. Can be tied to thwart for safety.* (B) *Old-fashioned fan-shaped seat and backrest. Common aluminum deck chair. Cushion only if passenger is wearing life vest. (He can rest his back against the thwart.)* (C) *Beach chair (low style).*

MISCELLANEOUS ITEMS

Personal items include toilet paper, suntan lotions, kleenex, towels, sunglasses, and visor hats. Complete raingear is a must along with some dry clothes, extra sweaters, or jackets depending on the weather conditions and temperatures.

A good camp or hunting knife can be worn on the belt and has a thousand uses. A cigarette lighter can be included in the first aid kit in case your personal one flips overboard or becomes wet. Bring along plenty of insect repellent and, if you buy it in aerosol cans, make sure the spring release works (many don't and are useless).

Cameras, binoculars, and other sensitive equipment should be carried in inflatable SPORTSPAC seal-tight waterproof and dustproof plastic bags. They should be stored in the canoe within reach of each paddler.

That's about it for the basic accessory list. You can ad lib from here for your own safety, convenience, and comfort. The choice of clothes is very important and the climate and conditions on the trip should be considered. Remember it is better to take along gear that you will not use rather than have to go without. Your canoe will carry a lot for you.

CANOE SAILING RIGS

There is quite a number of commercially built sailing rigs that are designed for specific canoes. Many of the manufacturers build in eyes, hooks, and brackets for standardized rigs that can be put up

Figure 26.   The Ron Canter sailing rig (from Canoe *magazine).*

STRAIGHT

BENT

Figure 27. Typical double paddle and double bent paddle.

and taken down in a minimum of time. There are also side panels or side bars that act as a keel for the canoe.

There is plenty of room here for your own invention. We have used the rig in figure 26 extensively and have found it quite fun. It requires only a bracket for the mast that is attached to the rear of the front seat. It was designed by Ron Canter and was publicized in *Canoe* magazine in March 1982.

DOUBLE PADDLES

For open water cruising and with two partners paddling in concert, double paddles will make the canoe fly along. Double paddles are also great for the single canoeist, except in narrow and confusing waterways. A simple cure is to switch to the conventional paddle until you are in the clear and then resume with the double paddle. Collapsible paddles are more convenient to store in both the canoe and the car. Buy quality and care for it.

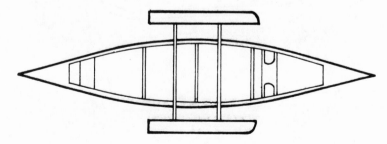

Figure 28. The Grumman stabilizing pontoons attached to canoe.

SAFETY PONTOONS

With variations there are a number of attachable bracketed pontoons that can be used with almost any canoe for extra safety and stability. We have used the pontoons designed for our Grumman canoe (see fig. 28). When we are out in all kinds of weather trying to get good wildlife pictures, this rig is a great help in steadying the canoe for telephoto shots that demand a stable canoe platform. Pontoons also aid in the camouflaging process.

ROWING SEAT

Yes, you can row your canoe if you like. We use the Grumman clamp-on model in figure 29 for this purpose. It is great to use when we take the canoe into the Daytona Beach surf. My wife holds the bluefishing rod as we troll just outside the breakers, and I do the rowing. We can instantly switch to paddling if the situation calls for it. This seat, as mounted in the center of the canoe, is also great for use with the double paddle.

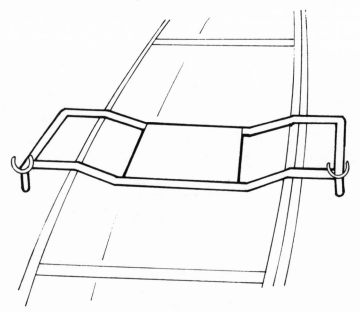

Figure 29. The Grumman rowing seat with oarlocks.

PART TWO

Mastering the Basics

Theory and directions are sometimes difficult to assimilate, follow, and remember; in this section of the book we are going to take you through the actual steps in mastering your canoe and its equipment. We will proceed step-by-step so that when you venture forth in the future you will have a sequence of events in mind. At first, some of the steps may appear to be quite rudimentary and almost obvious. But you would be surprised how often even the experts forget things, perform them in the wrong sequence, and thus become fouled up.

So, let's go canoeing.

1

Trip One — The Shakedown Workout

LOADING THE CAR

We assume you are well equipped for the first trip. You have all the gear ready to go and have the canoe in perfect shape. The car is filled with gas, and all equipment, including the lights and directional signals, is in good working order.

Before you start out from home to a fairly distant point, tell a neighbor or a good friend where you are going and when you plan to return. If you are going to a specific boat landing or a place where there is a phone, give this information to them so they can check up on you if you fail to return in reasonable time. You might get into trouble on the road or in your canoe, and this contact is the necessary link in being able to reach you or alert those who might be able to help you in case of trouble. Someone might become injured or sick, or one of a thousand things might happen to delay your return to base. Remember to let your home contact know when you arrive home.

Monitor the weather forecast beforehand and enroute in your car.

On a long trip, say a weekend or week-long cruise, you should include a portable radio in your baggage.

This first trip involves loading the canoe on the cartop carrier. You will be motoring to a canoe landing in this exercise. Park the car in the driveway if possible; loading on the street can be dangerous.

Two people will be taking part now in loading the canoe on the car.

The first step involves bringing the canoe from its resting place and setting it down alongside the car in a cleared area (see fig. 30). This is easily done by lifting the canoe, topside up, by the bow and stern covers and placing the completely empty canoe beside the car. Check the crossbar carrier, which is already mounted on the roof, for position, and check the tightness of the attachments to the roof or rain guards or door catches. Have available your bow and stern tie-down lines and the two crosslines that will fit over the canoe.

If your cartop carrier has a roll bar, one person can easily mount the canoe by lining it up behind the car, lifting the bow end high and, with the help of a second person, turning the canoe over so its bottom is skyward. Next, raise the bow and lead it over the roll bar;

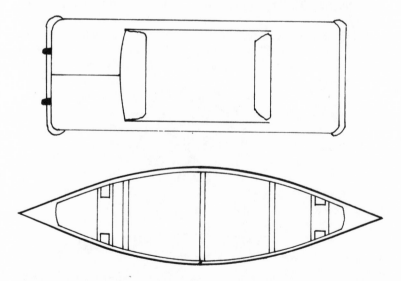

Figure 30. Before loading the canoe on the cartop carrier, set the empty canoe, topside up, alongside the car.

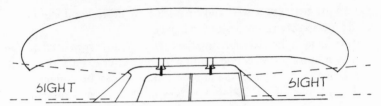

Figure 31. Position the canoe on the cartop carrier where it will extend evenly over the front and back of the car but will allow full vision from the driving position.

then gently slide the canoe forward to a position where it will extend evenly over the front and back of the car but will allow full vision from the driving position (see fig. 31). Pull the tie for the bow over and around the front bumper or attach it with clamps to the bumper, and then attach it to the canoe. Attach the stern line in the same fashion, pulling down tight so that the canoe will rest firmly on the cartop bars and will be even with the line of the car. This will prevent the wind from swerving the car in travel (see fig. 32). Next, tie in or snap on the two lines that secure the canoe to the mountings as tight as possible, and make sure they are properly centered on the roof (see fig. 33). Jiggle the canoe to make sure it is tight and resting evenly.

If you do not have a roll bar and intend to lift the canoe onto the roof, place the canoe beside the car with enough room to walk it

Figure 32. Tie down the canoe at bow and stern to styrofoam blocks. Hook the two cross ties into the car's rain gutters. To avoid wind thrust, line up the bow and stern exactly with the center line of the car.

to the roof when you lift it up. Two people can do this quite easily if the lift is done in steps (see fig. 34).

For cartop rigs made from four styrofoam blocks, it is best to attach the blocks to the canoe before the lifting; when you place the canoe on the roof, the blocks will already be in approximately the right positions—as far forward as possible and as far back as possible on the roof for good balance and equally spaced from the edges of the roof for centering. Adjustment can be made after the canoe is up on the roof before tiedown. Tie both the bow and stern tightly, and then tie down the two over-the-canoe ties that are either attached to the rain guard rails or to the roof between the door and the door sill top. A siren alert is a must for long distance travel when you will be parking overnight.

With the canoe now safely tied down, attend to all the gear you have selected and prepared for the trip. Make a list of the gear and

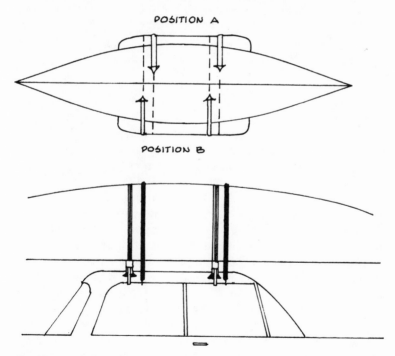

Figure 33. The lines securing the canoe to the mountings should be properly centered on the roof.

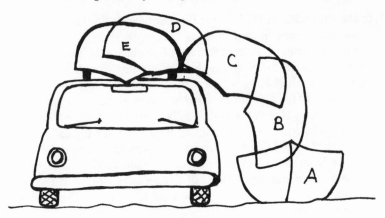

Figure 34.   Steps in lifting the canoe onto the roof. (A) *Both partners raise the canoe, which is now sitting upright with the gunwales toward the sky.* (B) *At a given signal, both turn the canoe halfway over and lift up about halfway to the height of the car top.* (C) *On the next signal, raise the canoe up and turn it over with the keel toward the sky. Move it to the car roof, touching the canoe gunwales on the outer edges of the cartop bars.* (D) *Slide the canoe easily along the bars and then center in position by adjusting from bow and stern.* (E) *Tie down as before.*

check it off as you load it into the car. (The forgotten camera? The film? The insect repellent?)

A typical list will include: two paddles and a spare paddle if you have one; two life preserver cushions; two life vests (check the buckles and straps); two sets of raingear in their pouches or plastic bags; food container; ice; thermos bottles filled and tightly capped; first aid kit; and little items such as an extra cigarette lighter, knife, aspirin, smelling salts, bandage, medicine, scissors, string, insect repellent, toilet paper, spare plastic bags for disposables, a compass if your trip is long or complicated, and a flashlight (even a very small one). Identification and your wallet should be in a waterproof container. Include pencil or pen and paper in case you want to leave a note either on your canoe or on the car where you park it. Extra clothing should be folded neatly and placed in plastic garbage bags. Cameras and other equipment should be carried in special tightly closed containers and should not be opened until ready to be used. All ropes, including stern and bow lines, should be in order and coiled neatly aboard so they will not fray loose in travel. Extra lines, such as anchor lines, can either be added later or lashed to the seats or thwarts.

Anything else? Make a check of what you wanted to have along and lay it all out by the car, loading it as you check it off the list, some in the trunk and the rest inside the car. Lock the car if you stop along the way.

ON THE ROAD

You're off!

Drive carefully, using your brake lights when you intend to slow down in traffic. If you plan to pull off the road, give ample warning. After going over a very rough road section or bad rail crossing, pull over and inspect the canoe position on the roof. Slow down at all rail crossings after giving sufficient warning to following cars. Don't travel over fifty-five miles an hour, less if it is gusty and windy. Slow down when you see an approaching truck.

Passing trucks can cause quite a sudden wind gust; depending on conditions, you should check the canoe if you have been buffeted by an exceptionally strong gust. The canoe *can* change its position on the roof, particularly if your cartop mounts are of the styrofoam block kind. Rain gusts and rain wakes from close passing trucks can shift your canoe without your knowing it.

When passing, give ample warning with directionals and leave plenty of margin around the passed car or truck. Always use hand signals in addition to directions, just in case.

Have a good up-to-date map available if you are going to a strange location.

Drive safely!

AT TAKEOFF LOCATION

We will assume for this stage of the trip that you will drive into a parklike area where there is a shallow beach for launching with a low docking area and a parking lot beside it. As you drive into the location, plan to park where you can be as near to the water as possible for launching the canoe. Later you can pull up to the dock for loading the gear and passengers. Making sure that the ground is not too soft, drive down to the edge of the water. You need to be able to back up and out to park the car after the canoe and gear are removed. Plan to make your moves as quickly as possible because others want to use the facilities.

Do not unload the car yet. Take the canoe off first. Untie all lines and fastenings from the canoe. If you use the roll bar you can slide the canoe down easily over the back of the car, turn it over, and then carry it to the edge of the water. With one person on each side of the canoe carrying it by the center thwart, walk it to the water and gently push it off. One person gets in with his paddle, and once shoved off from the beach, he heads the canoe to the landing platform.

Now you can unload the car and place all equipment in one place in preparation for loading either from the beach or from the landing. Hand a paddle to the one who will take the canoe to the landing if this is the plan.

The paddler in the stern brings the canoe to the landing and holds his end of the canoe away from the landing so that the middle of the canoe is tight to the landing boards (see fig. 35). It is not necessary to tie up unless both canoeists must leave the area at the same time. Equipment is then placed in the center of the canoe and the bow paddle laid against the bow thwart for future use. The gear is distributed so that everything is placed conveniently. The person still on the dock or landing parks the car in a designated spot, locks it, and, as prearranged, hides a spare key somewhere on the car in case of an emergency. The owner carries one set with him in his pocket.

If a passing boat causes a high wake, the canoe should be held away from the dock to avoid crashing and bumping until the waves

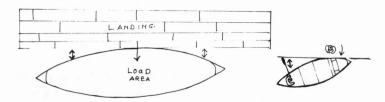

Figure 35. When bringing the canoe into the landing in preparation for loading, the bow and stern paddlers hold their points out from the dock, making the center of the canoe touch the dock or, if there are waves, to be as close as possible for easy and safe loading of gear. If both are on the dock instead of in the canoe, they can hold the canoe ends away from the dock. When holding the canoe toward the bow for the loading of the bowman, the stern paddler holds off with his paddle once the bowman has grasped the gunwale or thwart of the canoe.

subside, and then it should be brought in for loading. The bowman now enters the canoe by stepping in the center and immediately grasping the outside gunwale for balance. Both cushions are on the seats now, all gear is arranged, and paddles are in position for use. Off!

If a third passenger is included in the party, all the baggage is first set down and arranged with space left for the passenger seat to be placed forward of the center gunwale. The passenger is then advised to enter the canoe by the fanny route. He sits on the dock with legs hanging down into the canoe while both bow and stern paddlers hold the center of the canoe tight to the dock. The passenger then eases forward, grasps the outside thwart, and eases his body outward to the center of the canoe. Facing forward and grasping both gunwales, he sits down in the seat and stays there.

When the bow paddler sees that all is well and that the stern paddler has his paddle in hand and ready, he pushes his end of the canoe away from the dock. The stern paddler eases the stern from the dock and starts paddling on the left side; the bow paddler works on the right side. If a strong wind is coming in flat to the landing, the bow is turned into the wind as quickly as possible, and forward motion is started to keep the canoe from slipping back to the dock. If a passing boat threatens a large wake, wait it out, bow turned into the approaching wake. Bow and stern lines are aboard and coiled. Oh, did you remember to bring along a fifty-foot anchor rope and anchor and the bailer and sponge for mopping up water that can get into the boat? (We hope it doesn't rain on your first time out.)

When you have to load the canoe from a spot where there are obstructions such as rocks, ledges, tree branches, and the like, you may have to slide the canoe partially into the water on an angle from the shore and begin to load it from the stern. One way to do this is to have the sternman hold the canoe between his legs to steady and hold it tight. At this point the duffle to be loaded is nearby. When the sternman has taken his paddle and is still standing near the bow seat, you can hand him the baggage or duffle piece-by-piece, and he can load it properly. Place the heavy items on the stern seat where the bowman can reach them.

When all baggage is aboard and the bowman is seated, the canoe will likely sink further into the water raising the pressure off the bow so you can slide the canoe fully into the water. You can get in now by placing one foot in the center on the keel, between the seat and the back deck if necessary. At the same time you shove off, you can put one foot ahead of the seat, and then both feet, and sit down. It is a tricky motion to perform, but it can be done. Before you find yourself in such a situation, try this exercise from an easier place as a dry run.

Any time you have to enter a canoe that is partially in the water, take special care. It is not an easy task to walk down a canoe on an angle, even if someone is holding on to the upper end. Grasp both gunwales and, as you take each step, compensate with body balance to make the trip as smooth as possible.

The process and art of paddling and handling a canoe will be covered later, but the return to the dock and future loading is to be considered here for your return to home base.

If you are lucky, there will not be a strong wind coming into the dock, making it awkward and bouncy for landing when you return. Good docks are usually made in an L shape so that you can approach and land with the wind or waves in one direction or the other. If there is room it is better to circle around and land heading into the wind.

Make the approach to the dock straight in, keeping watch for other boats or canoes in the area. When all is clear, the stern paddler swings the canoe around flat to the landing but about a foot out from actual contact. Then with the paddle and later by hand he brings the canoe in to the landing boards. If the water is rough, both the bow and stern paddlers hold the canoe an inch or so away from the landing so as not to bump the canoe. The passenger embarks first while the canoe is held with its center as close to the dock as possible. If the landing is close in height to the canoe, the passenger places one knee on the dock, leans toward the dock with weight forward, grasps the dock with both hands, and raises the other knee. If the dock is six inches higher than the canoe, or more, it is sometimes better to swing around and sit on the dock in one motion. This decision is up to the stern paddler (captain) and depends on the physical abilities and experience of the passenger.

If you plan to leave the canoe at the docks temporarily, make certain it is tied at both bow and stern. Make sure it will not get caught under the landing platform or bang against the poles or supports. Sometimes it is better in a wind to attach a line to the bow with an anchor that has been lowered well out from the end of the canoe. This will keep it at tight angles into the wind and away from the dock.

When the trip is over, however, and everything is to be loaded into the car, the bow paddler lets go of the dock. The canoe is swung in for him so that he can reach behind his seat and place any baggage or gear within his reach on the dock. If the canoe is not too low, the passenger now on the dock can lift out baggage that is in front of the bow paddler or it can be handed up to him. The passenger begins to carry baggage to the point where the car will be driven for the canoe pickup.

The canoe can be taken from the water by both paddlers lifting one end at a time over the edge of the platform and walking it to the loading area. If the canoe is to be loaded from the beach where the trip was started, the sternman paddles it to the beach bringing only the bow as close to dry land as possible. The canoe is *never* dragged up on the sand with the stern paddler aboard or up an incline that would stretch the keel badly and bend the canoe. The stern paddler gently walks to the bow of the canoe while it is still floating and steps out. He then lifts the bow of the canoe forward onto the ground. Both paddlers can now grasp the canoe by the forward thwart and lift it ashore. They then switch to the center thwart and carry the canoe to the spot where it will be lifted onto the car top. Handled in this way, the canoe may never be scratched, punctured, dented, or bent out of shape—wet feet possibly, but the canoe is sacred.

Drive the car down parallel to the canoe. Lift the canoe in the same way that you did when you loaded it at home, and follow the same routine through the checkup of the tiedowns. Now reload the gear into the trunk and back of the car until everything is safely inside. Check the area before leaving and place all garbage in containers, or bring it with you to dispose of it at home.

All is well if you follow this routine faithfully—give or take a few variations because of the landing situation.

STORING THE CANOE

At home, the best place for any canoe is under cover, especially if it is made of strip construction, covered with canvas, or made with any of the modern glass or plastics. With the exception of aluminum, they all will deteriorate from sun, dampness, and rain. A set of brackets can be mounted into the ceiling of a garage of sufficient height so that you can drive the car with the canoe on the car roof to the

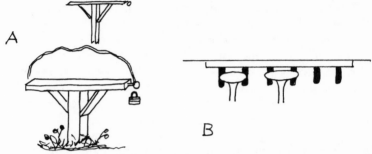

Figure 36. (A) *The simple T-shaped rig for storing the canoe is made from available lumber, preferably a 4x4 for the post and 2x4s for the top ledge and supports. Use treated lumber to withstand rot and termites. Brass screws will not rust like nails will. Place the posts in the ground so that the canoe support will be even and the supports will be near the canoe thwarts. You will need a set of two control straps to hold down the canoe for control in the wind and also to deter people from moving the canoe accidentally. A locking device will help to prevent theft.* (B) *A view of the paddle rack from above. Mount simple board, with dowels placed so that the paddle handles slip into position between them, on a plain board and attach it to the wall. The paddles will hang evenly and will not take a set.*

holding frames and then, using a pulley arrangement, hoist the canoe up and off the cartop carriers with ease. Or, take the canoe off the car roof and carry it to the sustaining bars in the garage ceiling.

A convenient way to house the canoe outside, not given a solid roof, is to rest it on strong T-base mounts. Set the canoe on the cross bars, gunwales down, and tie both ends to the frames so wind and rain will not dislodge the canoe (see fig. 36). A locking device is warranted here so that theft can be avoided. Arrange some kind of cover, such as a tarpaulin, and tie it down for security.

Never store the canoe on its keel on the ground or on a cement floor. People will walk in it, and dampness will attack it. An aluminum canoe can be stored in the open and mounted on boards at both ends away from the ground since aluminum is impervious to weather conditions.

Paddles should not be propped up against a wall. If made of wood they will take a set, and a bent paddle is an abomination. Store them in easily made holding racks (see fig. 36), or store flat on shelves or eaves out of the way, not near excessive heat or out in the open subject to weather. Items such as cushions, life jackets, and tarps can be hung under cover on rustproof wooden pegs or plastic-covered nails.

2

*Trip Two —
Small Lake Canoeing*

BALANCE AND HANDLING OF THE CANOE

Before you take off on even a short jaunt, you should know just how to balance a canoe whether you are in it alone or with a bow paddler. Yes, canoes are tippy, but this never needs to be a drawback if one or both of the canoeists are aware of how to keep the canoe in an upright, perfectly balanced position by compensating with body motions. The tippiness of the canoe is more apparent when a canoeist is alone since the canoe is bow light with all the weight in the stern. Even a simple paddle stroke will tip it slightly; the wind can also do its little tricks. When turned suddenly the canoe can tilt quite a bit. You have to offset this by body movement.

Sitting alone in the canoe, shove off from the dock for a few moments. Now, grasping the paddle in both hands held chest high across the canoe with the blade to the right, wiggle your fanny side to side and note how the canoe reacts. Lean over one side a little and then the other side and note the change of canoe balance. Move your legs around and note that even this much movement changes the canoe balance. Compensate with your weight.

With two aboard and with the shifting of paddling from side to side, the balance of the canoe can be maintained by subtle movement on the part of both paddlers. Strong strokes by both paddlers working the same side of the canoe will tilt the canoe over to that side. Strong strokes out of sequence will rock the canoe a bit and make it feel unsteady unless each paddler compensates automatically. It is not necessary to maintain perfect balance all the time, but if a skittery passenger is aboard, play it cool and maintain as much balance as possible. Such a passenger will be completely unable to help you. Always be ready to compensate for him if he makes any sudden moves. Remember, most passengers are not canoeists and do not realize the necessity of learning what you are learning right now.

Note the safe margin of canoe tilt. If you are in a bathing suit and the water is warm enough, move around and tip the canoe more and more until you either take in water over the side or tip the canoe over completely. (We'll take you through capsizing in detail later, but for now learn to keep things shipshape and as even as possible.)

If you are in a long canoe, say 18 feet, and are about to paddle alone on a windy lake, it is good to have some sort of weight up front (even a large rock) to keep the bow down and out of the wind. The more of the canoe that is in the water, the steadier it will be. Learn to paddle your canoe into (but just off) the wind direction so you can judge how far you can tempt a spill.

Quite often canoe balance is threatened when people start to move about in the canoe while under way. When you are alone it is possible to change positions or change seating direction if you are careful to grasp both gunwales when you make the move. Keep your body even to the canoe bottom in the turn around and sit down as soon and as calmly as possible. Handing gear or equipment from bow to stern, for example, requires some movement. Try to locate the gear as near center as possible. If the bow paddler wants an item that is near the stern paddler, he can hook it onto the paddle grip and pass it up to him or use the paddle as a tray when moving things back and forth. Both should not move at once.

When a passenger is with you, he can act as an intermediary in the passing of gear and equipment without getting up or throwing his weight around. Be ready to compensate for his movements.

All of this may sound tricky, but it will become second nature to you after a few short jaunts. Balance is needed in many of our everyday actions, and instant recovery of balance is often needed to avoid an accident or a fall.

LEARNING THE STROKES

Let's start with your paddling on the right side of the canoe. When not in use the paddle is always placed *in* the canoe, blade forward with the handle resting on the thwart in front of you. Never rest the paddle across the gunwales — it can be knocked overboard too easily. It is best to place it to the side of the canoe rather than in the middle since gear, cameras, or other equipment will be in the middle for your convenience.

Forward Stroke

Since you will be paddling first from the right side, grasp the paddle handle or grip with the left hand and grasp the paddle near the throat with the right. Hold the paddle parallel to the gunwales before placing it in the water (see fig. 37-A).

Correct posture is a must if paddling is to remain easy, comfortable, steady, and powerful. Correct fit of the paddle is of course the first commandment. Posture in the canoe comes next. Leaning too far forward and down to make the stroke becomes fatiguing. Keep the arms as straight as possible, but not stiff. If you bend the arms too much, you will have to straighten and then bend them to perform the stroke. This adds to the muscle action and is thus unduly tiring. Keep the back straight up but not tense. This will tend to keep your head up rather than down. A canoe trip is pretty boring if all you do is look at the floor.

Sitting for a long time, even on a canoe cushion, can stiffen up your bottom and back, and eventually you begin to feel the fatigue in the shoulders. Switch positions once in a while, if only to move your body a bit on the cushion. It also helps, too, to vary the position of the legs. The conventional paddling position is to put the heels close together under the seat, thereby lowering the knees so the paddle switching doesn't bump them. To vary the position, stretch one leg forward — the left leg forward when paddling on the right

Figure 37.   Forward paddle stroke. This is the basic canoeing stroke for moving the canoe in a forward direction. Both stern and bow paddlers use it. In order for the stroke to be most effective, it is made in a straight line back, not pulled alongside the canoe. In the beginning of the stroke (A), the canoeist grasps the paddle in both hands, with the right hand almost to the blade. He leans forward very slightly, reaches forward, and, placing the paddle in the water ahead of him, draws straight back (B). For the recovery of the paddle as it is raised out of the water (C), he feathers it to a flat angle to the wind and brings it forward for the next insertion into the water. That's all there is to it. A variation is the wide sweep stroke made in a semicircle instead of drawing straight back. This propels the boat into a quicker turn. If the stroke is made on the right side, the bow will turn to the left.

side, the right leg forward when paddling on the left side. For complete relaxation, place both feet forward for a while, and then return to the ankles-together position.

On long hauls when you are not near shore for a relaxing walk, stand up and stretch in the canoe, one person at a time, of course, and on signal to your partner. If possible, do not paddle more than an hour without some sort of respite and body stretching. A short trip ashore and a walk will do wonders to extend your strength. Now let's make the first paddle stroke.

To make the first stroke, the forward stroke, raise the left hand up and lower the right hand and move forward in order to place the paddle in the water ahead of your position in the water. The blade, controlled by the hand holding the grip, is at right angles to the canoe as you dip the paddle to the water. Submerge it to the throat now by pressing down with the left hand and guiding the paddle with the right. Pull back with the right hand and push down with the left (see fig. 37-B). The course of the paddle should be straight back for more power and better direction, not along the contour curve of the canoe.

Many paddlers start the stroke with a little extra push and then allow the paddle to travel backwards until lifting the paddle from the water. At this point, you turn your left grip hand and allow the grip to turn your right wrist so that the blade of the paddle comes out of the water flat to the surface, lowering air resistance to the forward movement. Your hands swing the paddle forward with the blade traveling close to the water until it reaches the original position for reentry into the water for the next stroke (see fig. 37-C). Repeat this exercise until it becomes smooth. This is the simple forward stroke. When more power is needed, extend your reach forward for a longer reach of water, and push down and back with more vigor throughout the stroke until it is time to retrieve the paddle.

Note that the canoe has now moved forward but is headed in a direction to the left. If you were to make several strokes you would travel in a circle.

J Stroke or Correcting Stroke

In order to compensate for any veering to the left you either have to switch your paddle to the other side of the canoe or correct the canoe direction during the last stage of the forward stroke (see fig. 38). To correct, allow the paddle to finish its work, twist the paddle to the vertical position in the water, and gently angle it out from the canoe while it is still in the water. This rudderlike action will bring the bow back to the right a little and maintain the course in the desired direction. If you correct too much, bring the paddle back in the water toward the canoe and the bow will react by swinging to the right a little.

Try some straight bow paddles now to get used to the action, and then take step two and learn to correct. This is a stroke coupling of two actions especially necessary when you are paddling alone.

Remember to pull your paddle back straight in the line of your direction, not hugging the canoe. It is unnecessary to touch the canoe with the paddle at all, even with the correction part of the stroke. This correction can be handled by holding the paddle out a few inches from the canoe side. If you are making only a slight correction, your thumb can touch the canoe gunwale and act as a fulcrum to the outward movement of the canoe blade in the correcting position. Lift

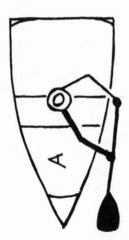 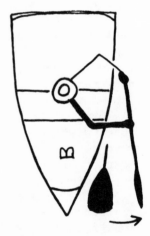

Figure 38. The J or correction stroke is part of the forward stroke. It is used for correcting the direction of the canoe. As you make the forward stroke (A) the canoe will tend to point to the left if you make the stroke on the right side. To correct the direction, turn the paddle to the vertical position while it is still in the water. Push outward with the right hand and pull inward with the grip hand. The paddle acts now as a rudder toward the back of the canoe (B).

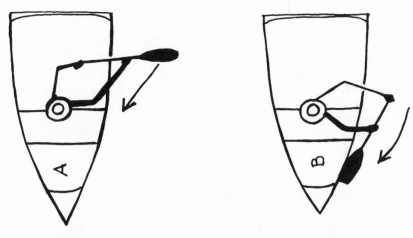

Figure 39. The angle stroke is a variation of the forward stroke. Insert the paddle into the water at a slight angle (A) and draw in toward the canoe rather than pulling straight back (B). This offsets the effect of angling the canoe bow to the left. It is an easy stroke for casual paddling and requires a little less effort than the conventional forward stroke.

the paddle from the water in the same way as in the power stroke and bring it forward through the air slightly over the water surface. Many canoeists, preferring to keep their paddles in the water under certain circumstances, will bring the paddle forward and then turn it flat again for the forward stroke. This is a noiseless and quiet way to handle the paddle when desired.

A subtle variation of this forward stroke is the angled entry (see fig. 39) and follow-through. Instead of entering the paddle at right angles to the canoe or flat on, angle the blade down about twenty degrees on the inside of the paddle. The stroke is completed with much less energy, but with less power, of course. It is a smooth way to paddle when full power is not necessary, and it is very relaxing.

When paddling with a bow paddler and constantly needing to correct, take one less stroke than the bowman and coordinate your tempo with his in order to have both strokes come off at the same time. If you are balanced in power, with the stern paddler using a trifle less energy, the canoe will continue straight ahead without correction. If you are both paddling on the same side of the canoe, much more correction will be needed unless the wind waves or the current is compensating for you.

Sweep Stroke

To correct direction the sweep stroke is often needed. Instead of the usual forward stroke alongside the canoe, the stroke is directed in a circle in order to accentuate the power in the turn (see fig. 40). The stroke is done by both stern and bow paddler. If a turn to the left is needed, both paddlers use the sweep stroke on the right side. This is done so bow switching is not needed, nor is a correction stroke on the left side needed by the stern paddler. The sweep stroke is often used in white water canoeing.

Switching Paddle Positions

It is recommended that the single paddler, and in fact both paddlers, switch sides often for resting and relaxation. Paddling on one side of the canoe for extended periods becomes tiring. Hold your paddle lightly—do not grasp too tightly as this becomes tiring.

To make the switch with a minimum of awkwardness, simply remove the paddle from the water at the end of the forward stroke, bring the paddle into position in front of you parallel to the gunwales about chest high, and switch hand positions (see fig. 41). Do not switch both hands at the same time since this would amount to

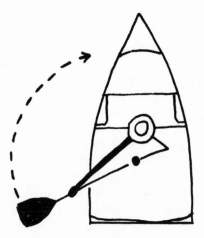

Figure 40.   The sweep stroke is often used to correct direction. The stroke is directed on the left side if a turn to the right is needed.

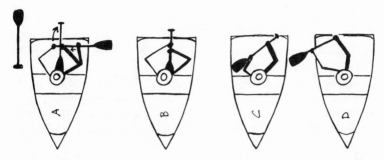

Figure 41. Shifting the paddle from side to side can be done easily and can become routine in a short time. Bring the paddle inboard (A), place the blade on the canoe bottom for the first try (B), and switch hands. For the changeover (C), lift up the paddle in a horizontal position. (D) The paddle is in position for any stroke. When you need to make a very quick change, bring the paddle into the boat with the blade up instead of down (A).

leaving the paddle in midair. The right hand leaves the paddle throat as the left hand holding the grip is loosed; while the free left hand grasps the paddle throat, the right hand takes the grip. Now make the forward stroke in one smooth motion, bringing the paddle forward before setting it into the water for the pull back. Make the stroke the same as you did on the right, forcing the blade outward from the canoe in the vertical position as a rudder. Switching back to the right side reverses the order for hand release of grip and paddle throat. It sounds confusing, but try it a few times to get used to the switch. If you are paddling alone and need speed or power against a wind, the fast switch is more productive than the correction; every correction in a slight degree slows down the paddling speed of the canoe. Both paddlers stroking and switching together is an effective way to grace the water with speed and a minimum of exertion.

As you will see in future trips, both the ability to correct and the ability to switch quickly and effectively are needed. It becomes second nature after a while to keep the canoe on course, especially in fast-moving water or where sudden turns are needed.

A slight variation of correction can be made when it is necessary to bring the bow back to the right while paddling on the right side. Enter the paddle slightly out from the usual angle and bring it back and in toward the canoe. This is a variation of the draw stroke which is made by reaching out as far as possible from the forward position and, after inserting the paddle in the water, drawing it toward the canoe rather than pulling it back. This stroke can also be made by swinging the canoe paddle in an arc or half circle. It is used quite often when turning the canoe abruptly.

The bow paddler aids in the effort with a strong forward stroke on the opposite side of the canoe, thus turning the canoe abruptly to the right. In case of a hairpin turn, the reverse paddling is performed with a quick change as you will see in a later session.

The Back Stroke

The back stroke is just what the name implies. It is used to stop the canoe as quickly as needed. It is done by both paddlers by inserting the blade behind their position and pushing it forward, making several strokes depending on the need for speed in stopping (see fig. 42).

A variation is placing the paddle in the water in a vertical position which will slow the canoe down. If more speed is needed for stopping, then perform the back stroke. This variation is also used when a slow speed is needed to go by obstructions or to slow the pace if another canoe is in front of you.

Figure 42. This is the back or reverse stroke, or even a holding stroke when it is needed to hold back the canoe and slow it down. With the blade flat to the current, insert the paddle toward you, push forward, and bring it out of the water. Repeat the stroke as necessary. This will slow the canoe's forward direction, stop it, or move it backwards. In order to bring the canoe straight back, both canoeists should be back paddling on alternate sides. The canoe will tend to move to the left if both are paddling on the right side as shown. When you need a quick turn, you may make a wide sweep stroke.

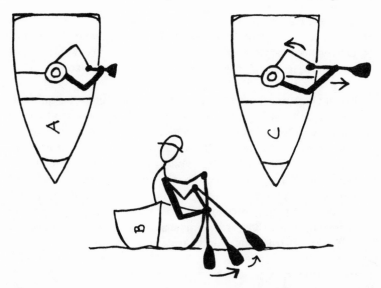

Figure 43. This is the push or pry stroke. It is used to move the canoe to the left if the stroke is made on the right side of the canoe. It is often used as an added correction when it is necessary to make a sudden turn, to fend off from an approaching rock, or to slide out from the dock. (A) Insert the paddle vertically at the gunwale of the canoe. (B) Push the paddle straight out from the canoe side. (C) Pull inward toward the center of the canoe. Lift the paddle out of the water and reinsert it into the water at the canoe side for the next stroke.

The Push or Pry Stroke

For the pry stroke the bowman simply inserts the paddle at the edge of the canoe. He then pushes it strongly outward with the shaft hand and pulls inward toward the center of the canoe. This turns the canoe smartly to the left. The sternman, wishing to aid the turning of the canoe to the left, uses the draw stroke which is made by reaching out to the side of the canoe and drawing the paddle in toward the canoe. The canoe will virtually turn in its own orbit (see fig. 43).

The Draw Stroke

The paddler, either bow or stern, uses the draw stroke in his solo canoeing and in concert with the bowman. He reaches out at a right angle to the canoe's side as far as necessary, inserts the paddle into the water with the blade angled flat to the canoe, and draws inward. Repeat as necessary (see fig. 44). Both the pry stroke and the draw stroke are necessary for quick movements in fast water.

Learn all of the above strokes by trying them out on a calm lake on a calm day, using buoys, docks, snags, or whatever so that you will learn which strokes to use at a given time under a set situation. A few hours of this kind of dry run is fun, and the experience will make you a very good paddler in short order. If you canoe with a steady partner you can synchronize all of these strokes and work in concert, with the stern paddler giving the commands for paddle strokes and switching of paddles. This will be necessary when you venture into white water or streams that have varied amounts of current, pesky obstructions, and sharp curves.

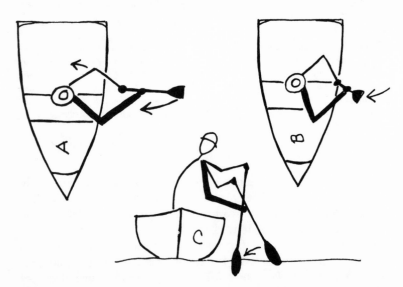

Figure 44.   The draw stroke is made in the opposite direction from the push stroke. Insert the paddle into the water (A) well out from the canoe as far as you can reach. With the blade flat to the canoe, draw the paddle straight to the canoe side (B). The action is shown again at C. This stroke is needed to bring the canoe to the right. It is sometimes needed to bring the canoe to a dock, to move the canoe to the right in order to avoid a rock, or to move the canoe for a different course when working in fast or white water.

The stern paddler should know these strokes, but with a steady companion in the bow it is convenient for the bow paddler to know them also, particularly the correction stroke. Both will enjoy outings more when they can reverse positions. After all, the bow paddler is only a power source on the straightaway, while the sternman is doing the steering and maneuvering — the interesting part of canoeing and the most intriguing. The bow paddler should have the same fun and experience. He should learn all that the sternman has learned. You never can tell when the bowman's prowess will be needed. In an emergency, he can take over the direction of the canoe, especially if he has to go it alone.

For those who are interested, we make a practice of teaching them at least the rudiments of basic paddle strokes, even if they go along as passengers. At a convenient stop en route, we invite the passenger, who may have never paddled in his life, to sit in the bow. We take a few moments off and put him through the various strokes. He usually thoroughly enjoys the exercise. Many of these people become paddling buddies for future trips, and some even buy their own canoes and join the parade (see fig. 45).

KNEE PADDLING

Although knee paddling may look awkward, it is a great way to offset fatigue from paddling from the seat position. Knee paddling is also preferred when paddling alone, especially in high waves or a stiff wind; paddling from the seat is more difficult when you have to fight the elements. Get down, brother!

For most purposes, the best position for the stern paddler is right in front of the stern seat, and it is an easy position to reach. All you need to do is to place the seat cushion down on the canoe floor and kneel down for the paddling, bracing your back against the seat. There are special kneepads and arrangements of pads for added comfort and specific conditions. These are available at canoe dealers or can be ordered from magazine ads and catalogues. If knee paddling is to be done only once in a while, the canoe seat cushion, or even the life vest, arranged for knee comfort, can be employed if adjusted properly for your use.

When you're paddling in a long canoe in extreme wind or choppy wave conditions, it is best to take up a position behind the front

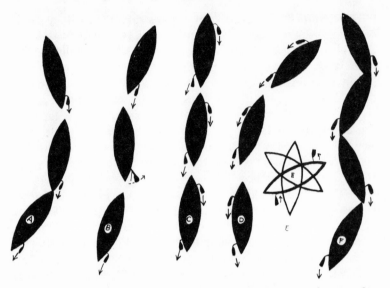

Figure 45. Read this exercise now so you can use it when you are in the canoe. Once you have learned it, you will be on your way to becoming a competent canoeist. The first stroke (A) is done by the sternman only. As he paddles the straight forward stroke on the right side, the canoe will tend to turn to the left. If he were to paddle on the left side, the canoe would turn to the right. The forward stroke with the correction or J stroke added (B), corrects the bow direction and thus the course of the canoe. If both canoeists paddle on alternate sides of the canoe (C), the direction is straight with the bow paddler exerting a bit more power than the stern paddler. Adjusting the relative power of both paddlers will keep the canoe going straight without the need for stern paddle correction. When both canoeists paddle on the same side (D), the canoe turns to the right if both are paddling on the left. The canoe can be turned in a complete circle within its length (E) by using the draw and push strokes on opposite sides. If the stern paddler switches sides at each stroke (F), the canoe will keep going straight even though it points to left and right at each stroke. The canoeist uses this to keep the bow from becoming a sail when heading into the wind or when he is in a hurry. The correction stroke tends to slow the canoe.

seat and face the stern of the canoe. The canoe will be better balanced, all things being equal (see figs. 46 and 47). The strokes can be performed from this position with a little variation of posture, since you are lower down now and the reach for each stroke is different than it was when you were sitting high up. The adjustment is easily made after a few tries. In the short canoe, the best position for balance is about in the center.

For relief on the knees, you can raise one leg and move your foot forward in a partial bend. Stretch your left leg out at a comfortable angle for paddling on the right side of the canoe. For left-side paddling, extend the right leg to a comfortable position (see fig. 48).

The Indians never put seats in their canoes. They paddled exclusively from the knee position, and so can you.

CAPSIZING AND RESCUE

You may have canoed for many years without capsizing your canoe, and this is commendable. But inevitably the situation will arise when, even for an unknown reason, you find yourself in the drink without any prior warning. If you hit an underwater obstruction and the canoe is the least off balance at the time, it will flip over. A sudden wind gust, a strong and high wake from a passing motor boat,

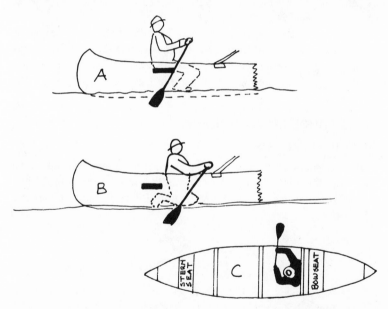

Figure 46. Note the difference in height between the position of the paddler when sitting in the seat (A) and when kneeling (B). Since the position on the seat puts the weight well up in the canoe, it offers less stability and more wind resistance. The kneeling position lowers the center of gravity and is used mainly for into-the-wind paddling or paddling through rough or white water. The paddler (C) kneels in front of the bow seat. This position is used for fast and white water canoeing. For the calm water position the canoeist kneels in front of the stern seat facing forward (B). With the weight placed as shown, the canoeist has better control in wind or in rough water.

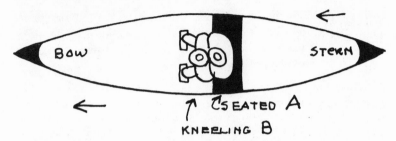

Figure 47. The single canoe with one paddler seated (A) and kneeling (B). In this position the kneeling paddler is almost at the center of the canoe resulting in better balance and control.

or any one of a thousand things can happen which will either ship a great deal of water or cause capsizing. You had better know what to do and perform well and fast.

For practice, put on a bathing suit and flip the canoe, swamp it a couple of times, and learn how to handle it in all kinds of situations. It's fun — and one of the exercises experienced in many survival courses and canoeing courses (see figs. 49 and 50).

SOME CANOEING SITUATIONS

Canoeing after Dark

If you are located on or near a neighborhood lake and intend to canoe on that water after dark, you should have no serious problems. But there are a few basics that you should keep in mind. Canoeing

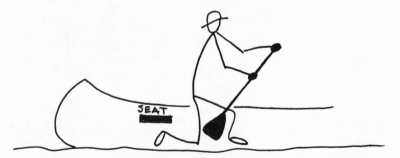

Figure 48. When knee paddling, raise one leg and move your foot forward in a partial bend to relieve pressure on the knees.

in darkness has special appeal and can be both safe and fun. Many of us who like to canoe after sunset include some fishing too.

If you have all of the preceding paddle strokes and canoe handling techniques under control, night paddling is easy. The only important point is to know where you are going and watch out for rocks, snags, and tree overhangs. The only rule is not to go where you cannot see clearly. When in doubt about snags and water depth, you can use your paddle to test the depth by deepening the stroke or pausing to stick the paddle down as far as it will go until you touch bottom. If you don't touch, you are well in the clear.

Figure 49.   The canoe is overturned and resting on the water. If this situation occurs on a lake with no wind or currents, there is little problem. If, however, the canoe overturn happens on a fast stream or river or in a high wind, the problems are magnified.

In calm waters, approach and right the canoe so that you can reenter it. The first step (A) is to remove as much water as possible by rocking the canoe sideways and then (B) to enter the canoe even though it is half full of water. Run the water out of the canoe (C) by bouncing at the stern, thus raising the bow so that the water flows backwards and out of the canoe. While it is impossible to get all the water out, much can be drained this way — enough so that you can handle the canoe and head for shore.

If the capsize happens in a wind or on a current, allow the canoe to drift with the current while you are on the upside. The canoe will not crush you then if it hits rocks or shoreline. Follow and guide it as well as you can until you can either touch bottom with your feet or beach the canoe.

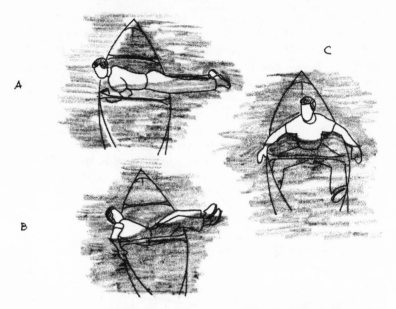

Figure 50. If the canoe is awash and current or wind make it impossible to drain it of water, the best way to enter it is by swimming over it near the center thwart (A), turning over the body (B), and then finally sitting in the bottom of the canoe. If the canoe contains flotation material, it will not sink. You are at least safe from drowning. Eventually the canoe will be driven by the wind to the edge of the lake or against the shore of a river or stream. At that time you can get out and lift the canoe to drain it of water. For safety, it is better to ride in the canoe even if it is being taken downstream at quite a pace rather than try to swim along with it or fight the current.

If you are canoeing on a waterway where there are likely to be power boats, bear in mind that they will not see you unless you flash a light toward them. At this point you hope they will slow down in passing. If you do not use a light, they will whisk by you and you will risk an upset or at least a very wet swamping — or perhaps an accidental crash. All power boats must have running lights. They are usually equipped with red and green port and starboard lights. Since you are not under power, these lights are not necessary. But some sort of light is necessary to identify you as a boater so that you can be avoided.

Usually boaters are alert to other boaters passing by them. At night, however, they have no way of seeing others except by a light flashed in their direction. If they slow down, chances are they will only dig the stern into the water. This makes a larger wake wave than proceeding at a faster pace, which causes much *less* wake when their boat is planing. They should slow down to a very slow (idle) speed that will offer no wake at all, but don't depend on it. Wherever you are, even quite a distance from their course, point your bow toward the wake and get ready to ride it out when it reaches you. When it passes, you can then proceed on course.

Learn to paddle quietly. There is no hurry. You are out for an evening under the stars to enjoy the darkness. If you know the area and its pitfalls by day, this is a great help. If you canoe in an area where there are confusing channels and many alternate routes, make sure you remember the turns or you can become lost very easily.

Solo Canoeing and the Short Canoe

In recent years solo canoeing has become a national interest. Many of the advanced designs for solo canoes are in great demand. These canoes are generally between 13 and 15 feet long; several popular models are only 10 feet long. They are easy to carry, portage, and store, and they are light to paddle alone. Many wilderness trippers use solo canoes. They find greater enjoyment this way. A lot of gear and camping equipment can be stowed in even a small canoe with only one paddler (see fig. 51). The solo canoe is not designed for two people. The seat is just behind the center of the canoe for balance. In many cases, the canoeist prefers to knee paddle rather than sit high up in the canoe, especially when negotiating fast or white water conditions.

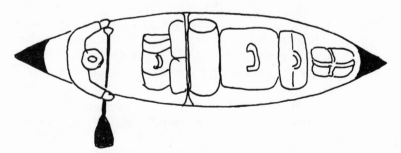

Figure 51. You can store a lot of gear and equipment in a solo canoe.

Solo canoes also make good duck hunting boats; in fact, they are good for all kinds of hunting and fishing, exploring, and photographic missions. The canoes are designed for fast travel and are not too steady, but the body movement of one canoeist is enough to maintain the required balance.

Canoe Fishing

Fishing from a canoe can be a lot of fun and much more productive than fishing from a motorized boat since the quiet approach is what seems to pay off. While it is quite a project to contemplate — paddling and handling a canoe plus working the tackle, netting fish, and all the other activities associated with fishing — it is not only possible but highly recommended. Many famous anglers canoe while fishing; that is, they use their canoes essentially for fishing. They prefer the canoe over the noisy powered craft.

Fishing alone in a canoe of 15 feet or longer is best done sitting in the bow seat facing the stern, the stern now being the bow of the canoe. The position nearer the center of the canoe offers better balance and control of the canoe in wind or waves. Getting to the fishing grounds is merely another way of using your canoeing know-how, but when the actual fishing starts, many new aspects come to mind.

The simplest way to fish from a canoe is to troll with rod and line. Simply rig up a spincasting rod and line, attach a lure to the end, troll it behind the canoe, and paddle along as usual. It is surprising how many fish can be taken this way when you least expect it to happen.

Set the rod in front of the thwart ahead of you with the reel and butt section behind and under the thwart (see fig. 52). The rod is now pointing slightly forward and out from the canoe while the line follows behind. A slow pace of paddling is needed; pace is dictated by the depth of the water and the sinking qualities of the lure being used.

This is the casual way to fish while canoeing at the same time; if nothing happens nothing has been lost. But from here it gets more complicated. If you intend to still fish or drift fish, you must use an anchor to hold you over a particular spot. Simply use your anchor line, coiled neatly aboard, and attach an anchor. This can be a five-

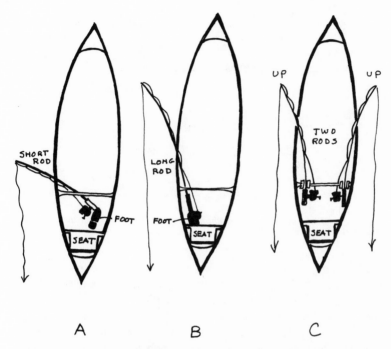

A   B   C

Figure 52.   Here are three casual ways of managing a fishing rod or rods while canoe-ing. They are pretty basic and require little extra equipment. For casual fishing (A), place the butt of the rod in front of the thwart with the rod under the thwart and pointed over the side. If paddling in rough water, place your foot on the rod butt. Set the reel drag well under the breaking test of the line in case you snag or a fish strikes. You can then reach for the rod and go into action. Hold a fly rod or extra long and soft action rod as shown (B), braced by your foot. The rod is under the thwart. To hold two rods upright with the butts resting on the canoe bottom (C), rig them with detachable wood braces. Several makes of rod holders can be clamped onto the canoe gunwales. The serious angler should use these instead of the rigging shown. Also available are vertical rod holders which are used in all kinds of boats and on all manner of rods. These can be attached to the canoe in an upright position.

or ten-pound rock, an old piece of steel, or a piece of concrete block. Attach the anchor line to the thwart next to your seat and drop it overboard when needed. When the line reaches the correct depth with enough slack to allow a wide angle of drift, you can tie it with a half-bow knot to the thwart. If you are fishing in a stiff wind and some waves, allow a good deal of slack so that the line direction to the anchor is not too vertical. Bait and drift fishing can now be done with ease (see fig. 53).

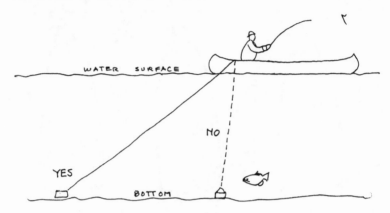

Figure 53. When dropping your anchor, allow enough slack so that the line direction to the anchor is not too vertical.

Fly fishing and spot lure casting can be done effectively from the sitting position. Lay the rods on the canoe floor and brace them forward against the thwart ahead of you. Pick up one at a time for specific casting needs. The tackle box should be readily available, either tucked under the seat or immediately in front of you between the rods. Best place for the landing net is behind you, between you and the deck cover where it can easily be reached without too much body movement. It is out of the way of rods and reels and lures (see fig. 54). If you use live bait, you can either keep it in a pail container or an overboard container. (Make sure you bring this aboard when you decide to paddle to another location.) A fish stringer is another good idea if you want to keep your fish alive. You can attach the stringer to the canoe seat and allow it to flow behind the canoe.

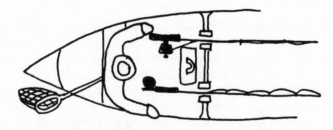

Figure 54. Place your landing net behind you where you can easily reach it.

Paddling while fishing sounds a bit confusing, but it need not be. You paddle until you reach the spot you want to cast from and either drift along, if the water is quiet and the wind down, or drop anchor and drag for a bit while casting to the shore snag, lily pads, or the undercut bank. After you have worked the area you can lift the anchor and move on, possibly casting in between paddling strokes.

When you want to play a fish out before landing it in a net, hold your rod high since the fish will sometimes swim under the canoe. You will then have to move the canoe by paddling with one hand and holding the rod with the other.

Netting is done while the canoe drifts since it is impossible to work the paddle and hold the rod and the net all at the same time. You'll get the hang of it and enjoy fishing from the canoe.

You can troll two rods and lines if you keep your wits about you. If you intend to cast one rod to the shoreline while trolling the other line, make sure the lure on the trolled rig is a floater when not moving. A sinking lure will snag the bottom when you stop moving forward.

Two fishing from a canoe is equally exciting. The bowman need not concentrate on paddling. He faces you, casting or trolling, while you stern paddle and act as guide. Or two can troll and paddle along in the conventional canoeing position, one rod on one side and one rod on the other. The possibilities are endless (see fig. 55).

If the bowman chooses to stand up for casting, you will have to control the canoe balance and guide him so that he will not be casting in your face on either the forward or the back cast. When it comes your turn to fish, the bow paddler faces you from the bow position and paddles as guide. Two can cast at the same time in either parallel casts or on opposite sides of the canoe. However, it is not recommended that both stand at the same time (see fig. 56).

Remember that casting requires body movement as does playing a fish and netting it. The lone paddler-angler will have to cope alone. The guide in the two man setup will have to do all the balancing compensations.

Canoe Hunting

Hunting from a canoe is a most rewarding experience. As with fishing, a great many sportsmen use the canoe primarily as a way

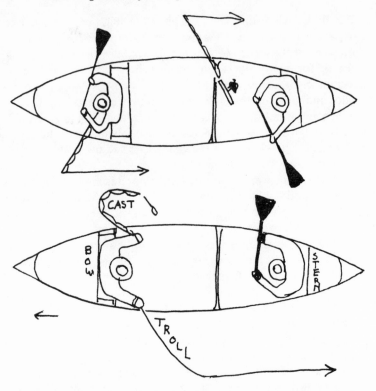

Figure 55. The bowman can troll or cast while the sternman paddles, or both can troll and paddle, one on each side.

of hunting. They are not necessarily canoeists in the purist sense. They just prefer the canoe for their purposes.

It is possible to drift down a meandering brushlined stream and surprise ducks and even geese. The canoeing hunter must be able to put his paddle down and reach for his shotgun in a hurry. The best position for the shotgun is braced against the thwart in front of you with no other gear in the way. You can make a simple bracket to hold the gun barrel against the thwart so that it will not slip and slide. Obviously the gun is uncocked in this position (see fig. 57).

The canoe can be used as a practical duck hunter's boat, even though it is not as wide as the conventional duck boat. Hunting,

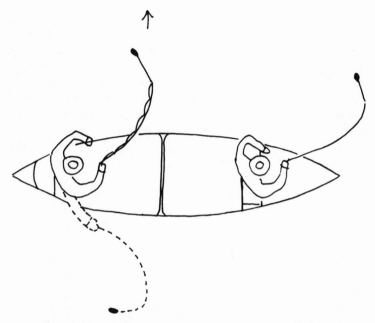

Figure 56. Both canoeists can cast at the same time in either parallel casts or on opposite sides of the canoe.

even with a retriever, can be effectively managed in a canoe. The decoys can be stowed easily for placing on the water.

There have been many deer killed from canoes. Early morning and twilight are the best times to slip silently along a lake shore or down a river. Deer come out to drink then and offer great shots.

Canoe hunting with a partner is less of a problem than hunting alone. Obviously, one person has to act as the guide, but you can

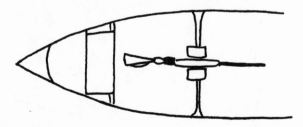

Figure 57. For canoe hunting, place the shotgun in a bracket holding the barrel against the thwart.

take turns as you would in fishing. While two can shoot at a flock of passing geese at the same time, they had better be shooting in parallel (see fig. 58). In fishing, the guide keeps the canoe crosswise to the area being cast to (as shown in diagrams), but in hunting, the shooter in the bow can either shoot straight ahead or at an angle. If he spots game behind the canoe, the stern paddler swings the canoe around so that the shooter doesn't have to fire over his head. The biggest problem is keeping good balance in the canoe when the shooter begins to swing to the target. It is up to the stern paddler to keep things even for him. The shooter's sudden movements and swings can be quite unsettling.

Bringing small game aboard is not a problem, but when it becomes necessary to load a deer or bear aboard, it is best to beach the canoe, bring the animal to the canoe, and load it as near to the center of the canoe as possible. If it is practical, dress the deer out first; the load will be of less weight.

Hunters and fishermen usually spend more than one day on their outings. Since they will want to carry camping gear and equipment, our advice is to select a canoe for the purpose—a wide, flat-bottomed canoe with the highest sides available and not under 17 feet, preferably 18 or 19 feet in length. The little one-man canoe can be hunted and fished from, but its use is limited.

It is not the province of this book to cover canoe camping; however, we can state that backpacker's equipment will suffice for your canoe camping needs. What you can carry on your back will be easily carried in any 15-foot or longer cruising canoe or flat-bottomed guide model.

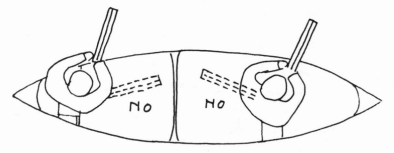

Figure 58.   The canoeists must shoot with their guns in parallel position if shooting at the same time.

Canoe Photography

The canoe really shines for photography and shows itself above any other craft. You move silently, easily, and can actually hide along the edge of the river or lake, moving along almost unnoticed.

We have used our canoe as a photography platform for many years; we have thousands of color slides of wild animals and birds as proof of performance. Our canoe is not a racing model. It is a flat-bottomed job with a fairly fat hull design, just right for stability. As we are not in a hurry, the slower platform is far more stable.

We alternate paddling frequently so that we both have the opportunity for good pictures. Quite often, however, the one in the stern gets as good a picture as the one in the bow. Here we have two chances at a rising heron, a flock of ducks, or an osprey flying overhead. Since we use telephoto lenses, we are both acutely aware of the need for canoe balance; we both use our bodies as balancing agents in the task of keeping the canoe even and steady.

We carry two cameras and a duplicate set of lenses, from wide angles to telephotos. They are instantly available in front of us—usually set down on the floor with the cushion of the inflated SPORTS-PAC bag to rest them on. If the wind is blowing, we are careful not to splash water into the canoe. We are also very careful in paddle switching not to dribble water on the cameras. In the switch we avoid the drips by reaching well ahead of the cameras in front of us.

The stern paddler is the guide again for most of the time. It is often necessary to turn the canoe at right angles to the normal course in order to get a good shot. When shooting static objects, such as trees, rock formations, or even resting birds, the stern paddler, being aware of the photographer's need for angles, handles the canoe by insight as well as command from the bow photographer.

We use a drag anchor very often even in lake work. We find it is better to drop anchor and drag a bit in order to drift into a shot that requires a particular angle. When we are photographing on a downriver trip, we use the anchor more often; this relieves us of the need to back paddle and frees us to take pictures without having to grab paddles suddenly in order to avoid a brushy snag or a sharp rock (see fig. 59).

When we are not actually using the cameras, we put them into their waterproof cases. We seldom wear the cameras with the neck

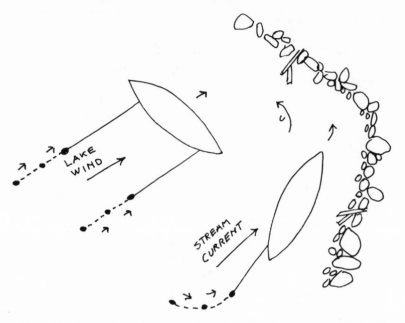

Figure 59.   When photographing on a downriver trip, drop anchor and drag a bit to drift into a shot.

straps; we prefer lifting them from the floor of the canoe for the shot and returning them to their cushion.

Again, as in hunting and fishing, maintaining canoe balance is crucial; sudden movements by the photographer while following a bird overhead must be compensated for by the partner in the stern.

Camouflaging the Canoe for Hunting, Photography, and Nature Study

This is strictly a creative proposition. Clothing is the first means of camouflage. Hunting garments in camouflage colors are worthwhile. In certain cases, it is helpful to color the face as is done in deer hunting. Camouflage hats are also worn.

The most important thing to hide is the canoe. This can be done by spray painting the inside and the outside with various paints in colors such as black, blue, green, brown, and yellow. Paint in strips to resemble brushy branches. In addition, depending on the kind of brush or grasses in the area you are working, actual branches and grasses can be attached to the canoe using duct tape that is easily removed after the trip and replaced later for another try. Both horizontal branches and vertical ones are used quite effectively (see fig. 60). Just make sure that the branches are placed so that complete freedom of paddle movement is not impaired. Even the paddles should be painted, since they are the only moving part of the outfit that would be spotted by wildlife.

Cover the thwarts as well. Use old carpet and wrap it on with a strong string. It is also a good idea, especially with an aluminum canoe, to use the rubber gunwale guards designed to soften the noise made when the paddles come in contact with the gunwales (see fig. 60).

Another method of softening noise and adding to canoeing comfort is the use of indoor-outdoor carpet cut to fit the canoe bottom and removable for portage. It adds little weight and much comfort including the removal of glare.

Figure 60. For camouflage when hunting, spray paint the canoe in strips to resemble brushy branches. Attach branches and grasses to the canoe with duct tape.

Multicanoe Outings

Canoeing need not be a solitary endeavor or even a two-person adventure. It can be a lot of fun to join a club, form a club, or at least arrange for compatible people to get together for a day's outing. While this informal arrangement is good, it is always better to be organized so that no one gets the idea that the leader is on an ego trip when he gives arbitrary orders. The club trip is under the direction and protection of the leader or guide, and those in the organization are expected to follow his direction, recognize his authority, and respect his advice.

In even the informal gathering of a fleet of two or more canoes, one person should be the leader, especially if he is more familiar with the watercourse than the others or is a more experienced canoeist. Since with more people and more canoes, more things can happen, it is up to someone to watch over the flock even though those present are equally aware of each other.

If one canoe lags behind the others and experiences some kind of trouble, the others will not know about it. The problem could be anything from a heart attack or a snake bite to a capsize. Either the next to the last canoe should lag behind within sight or the leader should hold up the flow until they catch up. If the lagging canoeists want to go ashore or pause for some reason, they should advise those in the canoe ahead of their intentions. Even so, the group should not go too far ahead of them.

Same goes for the lead canoe. It should not get too far ahead of the other canoes except when a photographer wants to get the lead ahead of the others in order to take pictures of birds or animals undisturbed by the rest of the group.

The leader should at least converse with the others from time to time, suggesting a pit stop at an area he knows will be large and safe enough for a multiple landing. Lunch stop can be arranged by communication after a few hours of paddling. Even the best of us want to get out and stretch our legs, relieve ourselves in the private confines of the backwoods, and just wander around to get a look at the countryside, taking pictures perhaps of wildlife, close-ups of old trees, and assorted group shots.

None of this direction need be arbitrary. The only time that arbitrary direction is needed is in the cast of a portage, rather than risk paddling through dangerous water, going ashore during a storm, or staying together in rough water. If a storm is approaching, everybody sees it coming, but some will want to extend the trip rather than turn back. They can either return with the group or go it alone. In a canoe club, going alone is a no-no; those who choose to do so will likely not be asked back again on a group trip.

The leader of the party should have aboard adequate first aid equipment, spare paddles, spare raingear, and spare food or water. At least he should see that the individual canoes are "fully found" or have aboard complete gear and needs for safety and comfort. In the case of an accident or sudden illness, it should be paramount to everybody that the trip be stopped and all hands help the one in jeopardy.

While all this seems obvious, it is best that all understand that they are *in a group*, and the success of the trip depends on the safety of all members of the group. When all goes well, the next trip is planned then and there. All at once there is the nucleus of a small club.

The canoes should pace the travel. In a downstream run, for example, they should give each other ample room for moving about the confines of the river. Some are more adept at negotiating curves, snags, and fast stretches than others. In this case, if there are two canoeists who are experienced, one stays behind the group while the other leads. If the lead canoeist decides to portage or line the canoes around a particularly difficult run that he considers to be too hard for beginners, he states this; it is up to the others to comply.

It is not necessary for all canoes to stay in the same position in the line. Allow canoes to move back and forth in the line and make allowances for pacing so that there is never worry of colliding.

At landings, the first ones out can help the others to bring in and tie up their canoes, help the canoeists to land easily, and bring ashore needed supplies for a picnic, for example. A kind of potluck exchange of food unites the group and makes friends out of strangers who might be coming along for the first time.

The leader of the club, the group captain, or someone whom everybody respects should see to it that all canoes are ashore after the trip and loaded on cars properly. A traveling caravan should return to the meeting center from which the party started out at the beginning.

CANOEING WITH THE HANDICAPPED

The crippled and the handicapped can certainly enjoy canoeing once they have been properly exposed to it by those able and willing to take them out for trial runs and to show them how to handle a canoe gradually. Through the years we have had this opportunity and have gladly given our time to people with all kinds of handicaps. As we mentioned in the Introduction, Dave, who does not have the use of his legs, has canoed over far more waters than we have. We also know a person who has only one arm that functions. You should see him paddle a canoe all by himself! Another friend is a heart patient. He has learned to paddle so that he doesn't become fatigued, and it is amazing how well he gets around. We could point to countless cases—the blind, the deaf, the dumb and combinations of all these, plus people with various deformities that limit their participation in most recreations. Many who can do well in a canoe are unable to drive a car, for example.

We have also worked with people who are mentally disturbed. We are always impressed how Mother Nature can have her magical effect on them after exposing them to a few hours under the sun on a lovely lake or placid stream.

Naturally, it takes people with canoeing experience and good equipment plus lots of patience to work with those who are less fortunate than themselves. But there is a reward that cannot be measured for those who do guide the less fortunate.

One of our best friends loves canoeing so much that he has made himself a beautiful all-wood model. He is almost blind, crippled with arthritis, and has a bad heart. The other day we spotted him canoeing on our favorite river . . . alone.

3

Trip Three— Big Lake Country

Oh, what a beautiful morning. As you look out from camp, the surface of the lake is glassy, reflecting the hills beyond. If you were to take a picture of it and turn it upside down, it would look the same. A canoeist is crossing the reflection now, carving a narrow slit of a wake. Beautiful. What a time to be out on the water . . . just like a mill pond.

Four hours from now that lake can be frothy with whitecaps driven by a gusty wind and piling up waves that can threaten your existence. If you are caught in this kind of water, beware. You'll get home all right if you observe a few precautions, and the exercise can be fun. Getting caught in this situation is one thing. Asking for it, by venturing out when you should be staying at home reading this book, is another.

You will feel like you are paddling in the pond near home when the weather is steady and the wind down. That is the time to venture forth. You should not cross a very wide lake leaving the safety of the shoreline a couple of miles from you. Unless the weather is going to stay fairly calm according to the reports, it is wiser to make at least a partial circle of the lake following the contours and keeping the shoreline within easy reach just in case of a squall or sudden burst of wind. If it does get rough and windy, you can head for shore, wait it out, or crawl along the shoreline under the protection of the trees and hills that deflect the wind upwards. It is always less windy near the shore, even if the wind is coming directly to the shore you are hugging; the wind carries over the tops of the nearby trees, cliffs, or hills leaving a partial vacuum.

Let's take a trip now onto the big lake and experience some of its moods. The slight breeze of the moment is coming straight for you. It will be best to launch and maintain the canoe with the bow pointed into the wind so it will not be blown sideways while you are loading or getting into it. Assuming there are no obstructions to your course, you can begin right away to paddle directly into the wind since the waves are small and inconsequential. No problem.

Let's paddle out about a hundred yards and travel to the left up the shore. Now you will be canoeing across the wind. You will note that the wind will continually try to push your bow to the right, toward shore. As the wind rocks the canoe slightly, both paddlers compensate with their bodies, somewhat like riding a horse. You compensate by angling to the left, a bit off shore, since the wind will carry you shoreward on the drift (see fig. 61). If your tour were to the right, you would do just the opposite.

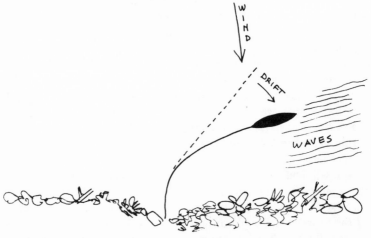

Figure 61. If the wind carries you shoreward on a drift, compensate by angling a bit off shore.

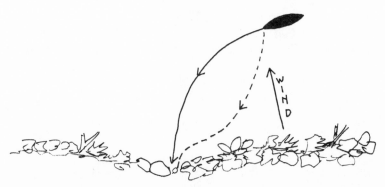

Figure 62.   If the wind drifts you off shore as you point your bow into the wind, compensate by heading more toward the shore.

Now, let us suppose the wind is gusty and shifts around and you want to return to your starting point. It will tend to drift you off shore even though you point your bow into the wind on an angle. So you compensate by heading more toward the shore (see fig. 62). If you decide to head directly into the shore now, you will find the wind at your back. It is an easy thing to ride in on it, and the run will take a short time due to the added speed given by the wind.

Okay, so far so good. But now, let's try the same routes in a very strong wind. As you start out from your first embarkation point, the wind is whipping in your face; but you want to go out anyway and have fun with it. As the canoe brings you farther from shore, the wind picks up speed and the waves become larger, faster, and choppier. A few sprinkles come over the bow, and each time you raise your paddle, it carries spray with it. Fun.

Your theoretical objective is a point on the other side of the lake, so let's head for it in this exercise. You will find that heading directly into the wind is tiring and bouncy, so you can tack just a bit off the wind direction either to the right or the left. With both canoeists paddling on the right side you can head slightly left. If you want to tack to the right side, paddle on the left side to offset the wind. You will hardly need to correct in this balanced situation, and progress will be more comfortable since your canoe is riding at an angle to the waves (see fig. 63). By tacking this way several times as you cross the lake, you will cover a few more yards, but the effort will be less. You'll get there.

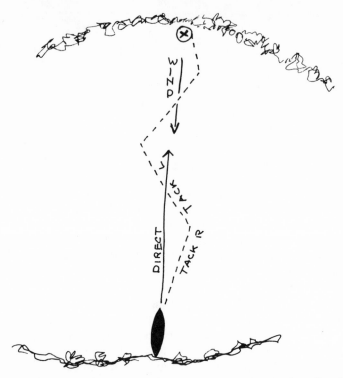

Figure 63. Tacking to the right or left as you cross the lake takes less effort than heading directly into the wind.

In a particularly puffy or stiff wind, both paddlers should kneel down presenting a lower profile to the wind. Even this little bit helps. Ever notice that in a stiff wind birds will fly very low to the water almost touching it with their wings? Take note.

So now, you want to return to your first base and must face the problem of canoeing with the high wind behind you. At first this seems to be to your advantage since the wind will help you get there quickly. The only "if" here is the wave height. Canoeing in a following sea can be difficult since the oncoming waves tend to try to push the canoe from side to side, and you will have to correct constantly. Again, it is often a good idea to angle your course to one side and then the other taking the waves on a slight angle for easier going.

In an exceptionally rough situation with high waves, the wind and wave action will try to force your canoe to broach, that is, turn sideways. Avoid this at all costs, for your canoe, and in fact even a small boat, will swamp very quickly when at the mercy of the waves. Both paddlers must be alert to this action and either correct or switch paddles to the same side to bring the canoe around and keep it on course (see fig. 64). Remember, since your canoe has little keel, it will tend to slide at the mercy of the waves and wind. You must compensate against both.

It is wise to get to know your canoe on a lake near home where you can practice a bit. Learning the ways of high winds and waves on a remote lake on long trips far from civilization is the last place to learn your capabilities.

It is difficult to bail out a canoe faster than it ships water over the side from slapping waves. Since you cannot paddle while you are bailing, the misery is extended. Do not let any amount of water collect in the canoe. Even an inch of water sloshing back and forth can seriously upset your balance. You then run the risk of turning over or tipping just enough for more water to slosh its way over the gunwale, thereby increasing the problem.

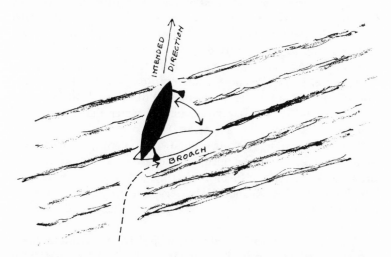

Figure 64. If wind and wave action try to force your canoe sideways, both paddlers must either correct or switch paddles to bring the canoe around and avoid being swamped.

All this may sound scary, but we are trying to acquaint you with the varied possibilities of big lake travel or travel on wide bodies of water, be they inland waterways, lakes, or even very wide rivers. Wide waters can offer glorious experiences.

The shallower the water, the quicker and more choppy the waves will become. When you are paddling over very shallow water there will be times that it might even be better to get out and walk the canoe rather than stay in it and paddle against the elements.

Don't avoid a hassle with wind and waves. Take off into it, enjoy yourself, and learn how to handle it. Someday that glassy lake you started out on can develop into a rage when you are out there in the middle, and you will have to figure a way to reach the shore dry and in one piece.

In the north country, summer is the time when most canoeists are about. It is also the time of squalls, thunder storms, and just plain high winds. Keep an eye on the weather and the clouds; if you are out with an inexperienced paddler, don't risk scaring him to death. Head for shore. Generally, you can see a thunderstorm well in advance.

There will be a period of absolute flat calm — the proverbial calm before the storm. Don't be lured by this glassy calm. Use that time to find a safe harbor in the lee of the wind. Bring your canoe well up from the water in case of a real blow, and tie it down to a rock or tree stump in case the wind wants to play with it.

It is fun to run the waves and be buffeted by the wind if this is your choice. It is quite another matter to be caught out in a situation you didn't bargain for. In the interest of safety, head for shore. It is better to miss a few hours on the water than to struggle dangerously and perhaps not make it in dry.

If there is lightning flashing around you, do not stand next to an isolated tree or out in the open. Certainly do not remain in or on the water in the canoe. If lightning strikes nearby, the shock can be felt through the water and can be very destructive. Hide under a clump of trees or in the bushes, or lie flat on the ground until it is over.

If there is no alternative and the wind is driving you to the shore, go with it rather than head for home against it. Wind dies down eventually; in the calm you can return, this time a bit smarter.

Sometime, just for the fun of it, take your canoe out by yourself when the wind is blowing and there are six inch waves to roll you around a bit. Start out straight into the wind and allow the wind to turn you, let's say, to the right. Paddle against that pressure and try to bring the canoe back straight into the wind. Let it fall off again and paddle across the wind, parallel to the waves, and note the motion. Turn more to the right and angle across the wind which is now coming more from behind you and the quartering waves.

Paddle now directly with the wind and note the difference in the wave action. Bring the canoe around to the left, and watch the wave and wind action as you work through the parallel waves. Finally, head into the wind again. You will have traversed every kind of condition and will have learned how and when to correct, wide paddle to make the turn, switch sides, and generally handle the canoe balance with your body. From then on you will be prepared for anything other than a gale.

Do the same thing with your partner in the bow. Note how it is possible for two in concert to cope with the wind and wave actions. Switch positions and let the bowman experience it too.

4

Trip Four—Gentle River Downstream

Now you can put into practice all you have been able to learn so far in an actual river trip. The gentle river will give you the fundamentals of experience that are needed for faster rivers and eventually white water canoeing. But first things first.

Our river is about a hundred feet wide at its widest and sometimes only about ten feet wide on the bends. The water speed varies from about one to three miles an hour. The river has its straight wide stretches, gentle narrower bends, some sharp hairpins, plenty of obstructions such as sunken logs, downed trees, and a few rocks and boulders.

In the slack water below the bends and turns we see generous floats of lily pads and tall grasses that tell us of shallows. Watching the water currents, we can spot ahead just where and where not to travel. We will experience the unpredictable drift of the canoe, learn to compensate for that drift, and steer a course that will offset it.

For solo paddling you can readily see that you will have to supply steering and power all by yourself. Spotting the course is just about the same, but coping with the turns requires more decisive action —more pronounced steering and correcting and much more switching from side to side. The starter canoe (13-14 feet) will react much quicker than the 16-18 footer, but you will have to contend with the current drifting you about.

We are going to negotiate a typical curve in a 30- to 40-foot-wide river. Current is about two miles an hour; due to water surface disturbance current directions can be seen quite easily. Note that the slack water sections of the curves have sections of lily pads, signifying shallow and slack water. The bends opposite them are usually rocky or contain snags and underwater rocks.

The current is going to swing the canoe in its direction. You will have to anticipate this and make your moves accordingly. Be ready to shift paddles from side to side; the stern paddler must be prepared to either switch or correct in his stroke.

At A, you are preparing to set course for the first curve stretch. The main current is to your left. Rather than follow it, you bear to the right since the current would set you into the bend (1) if you did not stay away from it. At B, you are still paddling on both sides and the canoe slips to the left since it tends to follow the current. The stern paddler corrects this and the bow paddler helps. At C, you head straight for the pads; the current wants to drag you more to the left. You are even with it all at D, but the stern will now be dragged to the right by the current. Figuring on the drift to the right you will head for the pads in this second stretch, pointing the bow into them. Note the paddle changes. Use the swing in the current at E and F, and then drift down to G. You are home free.

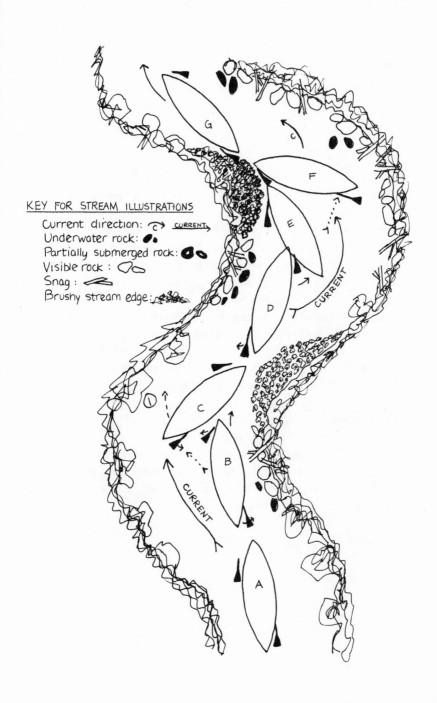

KEY FOR STREAM ILLUSTRATIONS
Current direction: ⤳ CURRENT
Underwater rock: ●●
Partially submerged rock: ●●
Visible rock: ○○
Snag: ⤮
Brushy stream edge: 🪨

This is a typical bend in the river. It is an easy one if you figure on the current drifting you and compensate for it by switching and with stern paddle correction. If you don't, it will take you too far to either shore as you go through. This will make it awkward and necessitate extricating yourselves from the brush and possibly bumping into some underwater snags and rocks. At A, both are paddling on the right side to center in the river. At B, the bowman switches to the left side. As the current pulls the stern to the right, the stern paddler switches to the right to correct the drift. At C, both are paddling on the left side to correct into D as the current now begins to pull the canoe to the left. Both paddle on the left side toward F and head into the lily pads as the current drifts the canoe stern to the left toward that underwater rock. The stern paddler corrects, the bow paddler helps, and you drift to G. Work the same way to H and correct to I for the end of the run.

You will learn that it is better to work with the current rather than fight it. Note how the canoe reacts to the water and learn to work with it for a smooth ride with a minimum of paddle changes and awkward movements.

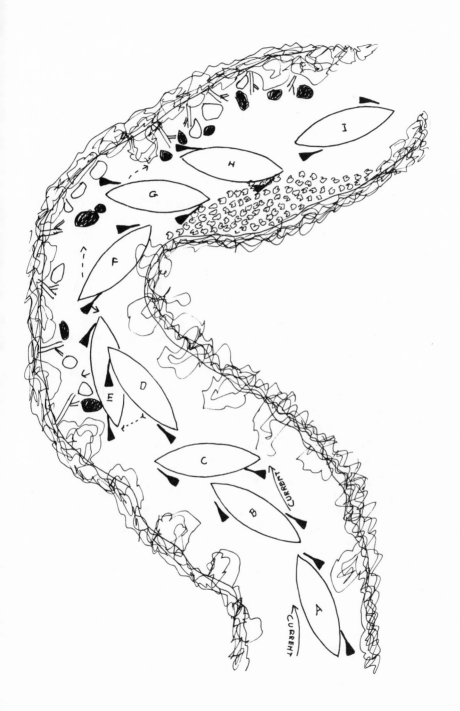

Here we try a tight bend in the river where the current becomes a bit faster. Note the moves to compensate and drift using the current in the right directions. You must avoid being drifted or pushed by the current to the right side of the upper or first bend and to the left in the second part of the bend. At A, you are paddling both sides. At B, begin to correct as the current slides the canoe to C. Keep the bow headed for the left side of the river and allow the canoe to drift easily to D. Drift to E as the sternman shifts to the left side. To avoid being pushed into the corner, head for the point at F. The current will act on the stern at G and H, but keep that bow in to the point. The drift to I is easy. To avoid being pushed against the left bank, head the bow into the shallow with its pads. At J, relax the direction and slide to K. Straighten out at L for the next part of the trip.

Going through such water will show you that it is always a good idea to work with the current. Allow it to take you along, but at the same time slice through the pressures to head you in the right direction. Watch the current lines on the water surface. They will tell you just about what is going to happen to you ahead. You can then decide just how to work the current in the most efficient way for a smooth ride.

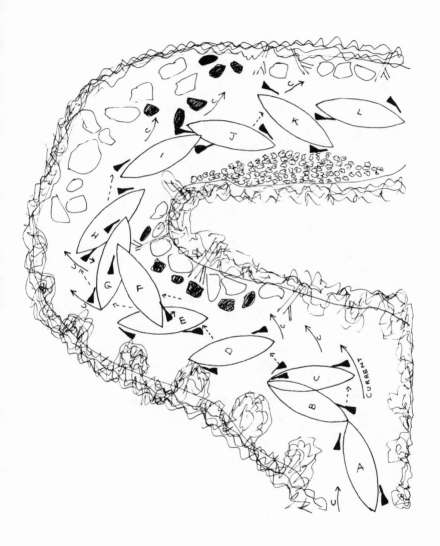

This is a typical shelving riffle where the river widens, but don't take that shallow for granted. It is rocky and full of snags. The other side, too, is rocky and snaggy; you will notice that the current is pushing constantly against that left side. You must avoid being pulled into it or the stern of the canoe will scrape the edges. In a faster current it could upset you. This is easy water as long as you keep that bow pointed toward the shallows, even touching bottom once in a while as an alternative to being pushed against the far shore. At A, both are paddling on alternate sides. At B, with the current beginning to act on the stern, the stern paddler corrects and the bowman paddles strongly forward. At the drift to C, the stern paddler switches to the left and the bow paddler to the right as the canoe drifts well to D. There, both paddle on the left side to hold the easy drift downstream. At E, the current still pulls the canoe stern so the stern paddler switches to the right. The drift to F calls for both to paddle on the right side down to G where the deep water narrows. At H, go straight and easy; you are in the clear.

This can be an easy ride, not a hassle, if you anticipate your moves and account for the drift that is going to take place. Use the current—don't fight it.

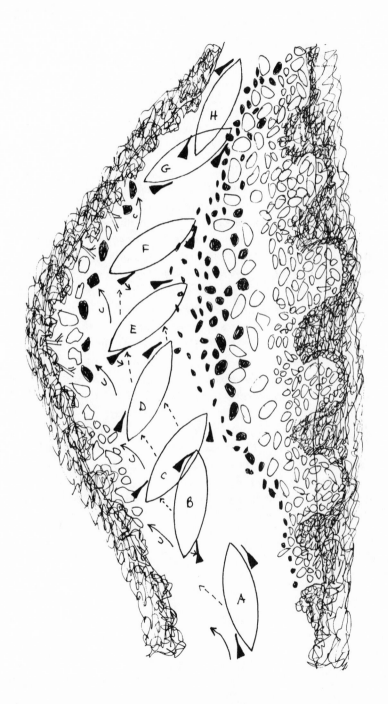

This can be a hassle, but let's try to make it simple by taking it easy on the way down, using both paddles to slow the trip, and watch the angles. Take a good look at it before moving forward. Note those underwater rocks. If the water is not clear enough to see them, watch the ripples on the surface. They will tell you all you need to know. Ahead, the opening begins to narrow and has snags and rocks; you will need to decide how you are going to make it through. At A, negotiate the rock (X). At (B), when you feel the canoe swing to C, the stern paddler switches to the right side. At D, the current will drift you nicely past the rock (Y). The stern paddler and bow paddler both backstroke to slow the pace. At E, begin to sneak through the narrow opening at a good angle to the snags. The stern paddler quickly switches to the right side and paddles hard to turn the canoe to the left as the bow paddler fends off the snags to his left. With the current now pulling you to the right, you are in the clear. Now, that wasn't hard, was it? Just take your time in these situations. There is no hurry and it is fun to figure out the angles — somewhat like playing pool. You will need to know when to switch sides. The stern-man should give the directions to the bowman since he relies on the bow strength for the movements.

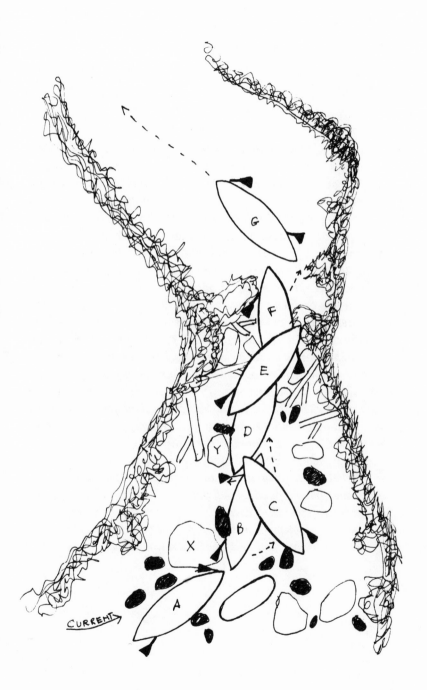

CURRENT

This one can get you into trouble. You can get caught up in the snag, hit by it, or possibly capsize the canoe if you don't take it properly. As you approach it, you can see how much space there is between the water and the branch and what you have to do about it.

First, both paddlers back paddle as you slowly approach the snag overhang. Do not stand up in the canoe or reach for the snag as you approach it. Don't try to wrestle with it. *Avoid it easily by bending down in your seat and keeping your head down until you are in the clear. The sternman can advise the bowman to bend down lower as the approach is made. Since he can see the amount of clearance, if any, he can advise the bowman to get down on his knees. In this case, the bowman brings his paddle inboard. When the bowman has passed under the overhang, the sternman tells him. He can then put his paddle in the water again for any needed control. If the current is fast, he is now free to back paddle on both sides with quick switches so the canoe doesn't travel too fast for the sternman. The sternman is down as low as necessary; when the overhead danger has passed, both are in the clear.* Do not bend backwards when approaching or going under an overhang because it will put you off balance. *If you are not low enough to the canoe, the snag can scrape you and possibly pull you overboard or force you to tip the canoe; you will then have lost control of the whole operation.* B *shows the problem from behind as you go through.* C *shows it sideways with both paddlers bending down for ample clearance.*

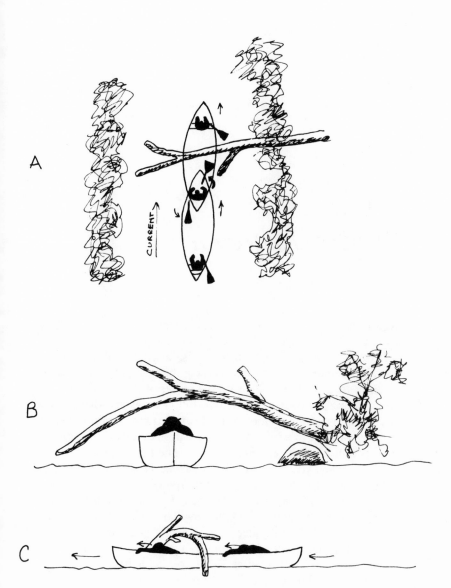

A

CURRENT

B

C

5

Trip Five — Gentle River Upstream

We will return to base now, working our way upstream through the same problems. Let's see how to handle them.

In one sense, paddling upstream is easier as far as accurate manipulation of the canoe is concerned; the current vagaries will be easier to face and overcome with the power of the paddle and you are initiating the course rather than following as you did to some extent while drifting. While in the downstream run, you were able to relax and drift to a certain extent; the upstream trip is one of constant pressure and direction. The only time the current will cause trouble is when you point too far off from it and allow the canoe to be swung in the direction it dictates. You will, however, note that the canoe will tail wag a great deal at first while you are trying to keep your point accurately into the flow. This swinging will not only hold you back but could place you in a spot you didn't figure on.

Being near the center of the canoe is a great help. If you are knee paddling it will seem much easier to keep your balance.

In the next exercise — paddling back upstream — your short craft will have the advantage. But two good paddlers in a longer canoe can do just as well.

In this exercise both paddlers will have to change sides at the same time, in some cases quite quickly, in order to make the turns needed in time to avoid trouble. The draw stroke, the back stroke, in fact all strokes will need to be worked in concert for a smooth ride up the currents.

Many of the rivers in Florida and in similar flat country are of the type you have just mastered. They are pretty rivers and each turn is to be savored once you have control of the canoe. When two are paddling, a kind of psychic understanding of paddle assignments develops in addition to the directions from the stern paddler. You will have learned of the vicissitudes of the current in both directions and your particular canoe's reaction to them. You may have not always made it through perfectly. The current was misjudged for its strength; the drift or tail wag of the canoe was not snubbed quickly enough and controlled. You may have to sharpen up your pointing a bit closer to allow for thrust and swing on all types of curves. Your judgment in going through tight squeezes between rocks or downed trees may have to be sharpened by spotting the problem well ahead of time.

Work several of these waters before going in for faster and tougher waters. It is delightful canoeing. You'll want to bring a passenger along for the ride soon, so have it pretty well under control. All it takes is practice, and each day on this kind of water can and will be a delight.

Give other canoes plenty of room. Don't expect that they will reciprocate in time. They may be rank amateurs or unmindful and inconsiderate. When paddling in a group keep your distance—and be aware of the canoe behind you as it might climb up your back!

This is the same stretch of river we went down on page 115. You will notice, however, that the technique of upstream paddling and upstream negotiation of the water is a bit different than before. The current will constantly buffet you to the right or left; you should steer as much as possible in a way that this will not happen. By studying the water in the following trips, you will get to know just how these current pressures work on your canoe. Although you will work a bit harder paddling against the current, it will actually be much easier since you will be more in control. Since you are moving against the current, you can use it to your advantage and slip right over it.

At A, you begin to try the turn. The current at B will try to swing the canoe around; the stern paddler corrects against it while the bow paddler adds forward push. At C, keep your nose straight by alternate side paddling. At D, head for the very edge of those snags rather than risk being pulled into that right eddy. You are heading right into the current at E, and at F you are in the straightaway. Easy? Watch those currents and keep control of the bow direction.

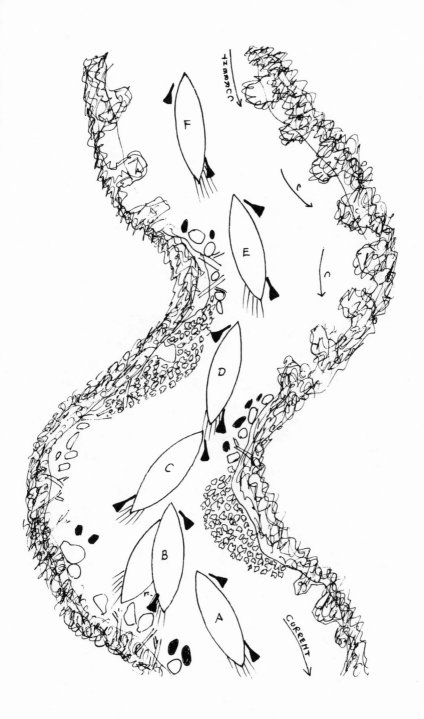

This is the same water as in your downstream trip on page 117. It is not a difficult run, but it is one where you can get used to paddle switching and correcting. Either the stern paddler gives the order to the bowman, or better yet, both realize at the same moment which way to go and what to do to accomplish it. Again, reading the water ahead of time can save a lot of wrong action, wrong direction, and overwork. Paddling upstream requires that you both operate with as much proficiency as possible; on a long run, those who arrive at the destination with a minimum of fatigue have really earned the title of canoeist.

At A, you have just turned to negotiate the first part of the bend. To make an easy turn, the stern paddler shifts to the left side and, both paddling left, the canoe goes right over the current. Had you chosen the right side of the river, you would have had to buck the strongest current. At B and up to C where the current will tend to pull your stern to the right, you correct. At D, you do the same; both paddlers paddle in even force to keep the canoe bow right into the current. At E, you are both on the right to offset the current which is now stronger on the right side. At F, all things are equal for an easy run upstream to the next bend or problem.

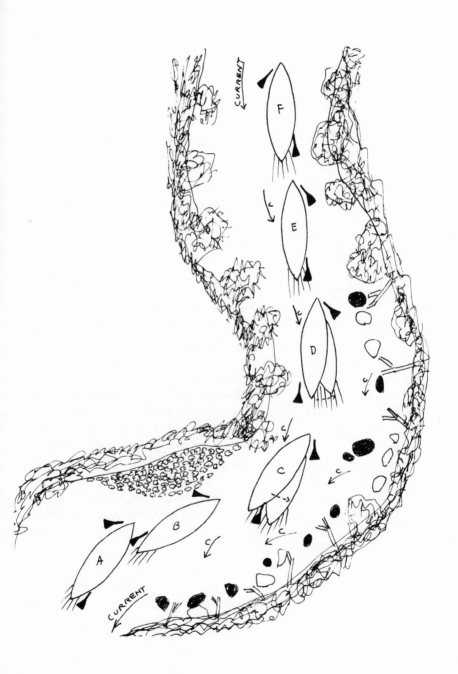

You are headed upstream now on the same water as on page 119. There is a sharp bend in the river, a lot sharper than in the previous exercise. You will need to perfect this kind of bend since it is quite common in faster streams; both upstream and downstream work must be done accurately and will sometimes require quick decisions under full power.

At A, we start with alternate side paddling and allow the current to take the canoe to the left into the shallows. The main current fans out to both sides. You do not want to or need to work the canoe through the faster, heavier current over to the right where there are rocks and snags to contend with. At C, the stern paddler turns the canoe to the left and the current tends to take the stern and twist it out to the right. This takes a slight correction while both are paddling hard upstream. At D, the correction is needed again; both paddle on the right side for ease. They continue to E almost in the center current, and the bowman switches to the left side. At G, the stern paddler corrects after switching from the left side to straighten out the canoe for what is to come. On a stream that is moving along well this kind of paddling can be a delight; you can easily spot your course and work your way up without too much effort, watching the effect the current has on the canoe and correcting either from the bow or stern, or both. You will learn to work as a team to prepare for the waters that you will be working next. The faster stretches, where cooperation and double vision are a must, will be more difficult to confront.

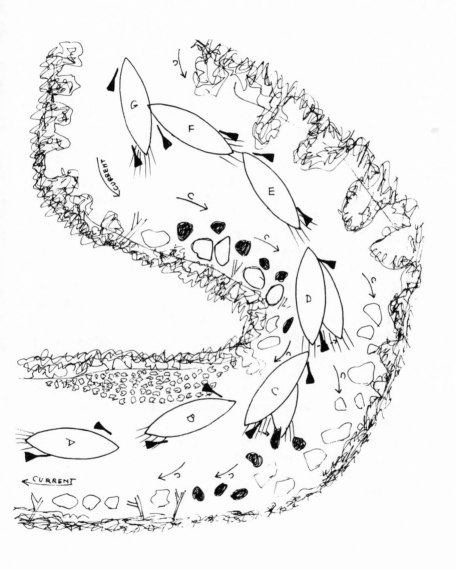

Here we return to the shelving riffle, but this time we are going to take the canoe up through the currents in as easy a way as possible. A look at the water from A shows a thin layer of water coming down and flowing into the pool. The main current goes down the center pushing its way against the right bank and those submerged rocks and shore snags. This is an area you want to avoid at all costs, especially in a situation with much faster water. At A, you are alternate side paddling. The stern paddler shifts to the right side and corrects so the bow is headed right across the water coming from the shallows of the sand and gravel bar which causes the riffle. At B and C, you are alternate paddling again, just to keep the nose up against the flow, and watching the effect of the current. D shows the action of the current on the canoe stern as it tries to pull it to the right, so correction is necessary. Staying in the left of center current, you have minimized the effort needed to run through this water. At E, both are paddling on the left side. The next vista will offer something new.

This kind of water is very common in northern rocky rivers and large snaggy streams suitable for canoeing. There is a lot of so-called waste water in large streams, especially at low water; spotting the direction of the current is sometimes tricky. If you note just how the current is working on this stretch, you can use it as a model for future runs that are more complicated. This is also good fishing water. Poling along slowly here and allowing the bowman to cast a few flies might give us all something good for supper.

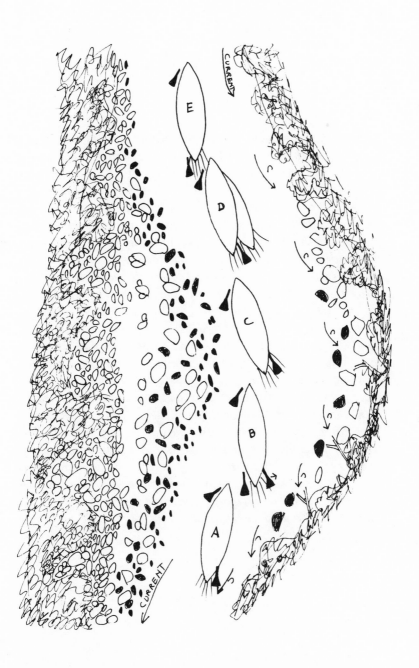

Here's that snag again; but this time we are going to take it going upstream. As the current is slipping by here at a slightly faster pace, your accurate steering and bow paddling must be "tight" as you head into the trouble spot. At A, you are alternate side paddling. As you look ahead to where and how you must come though the narrow passage, guide the canoe at B slightly to the right of the hole so that you can use the current to move you to the left a bit to angle into the passage. The bowman back paddles to slow the canoe; the stern paddler switches to the left side and also holds back to let the canoe go by itself through the passageway. Since the bow paddler is ready to fend off the rocks, the stern paddler has to exert himself to generate enough power to go through. Once through, the stern paddler switches to the right side and both paddle hard to rise above the passageway and to avoid being swung around by the currents. As you are alternate paddling at E, look ahead for a course at the space between the visible boulders, and look at the sunken rocks. If the rocks are not causing a ripple on the surface, you can usually safely travel slowly over them; a sizable wake behind them will show that they are almost breaking the surface. A lot of study should be devoted to measuring the morain of water over these underwater rocks. When the water is clear, you can be fooled as easily as when the water is cloudy or discolored. Judge the depth of water over the rocks by the disturbance they make in the current. No problem — you'll get used to it.

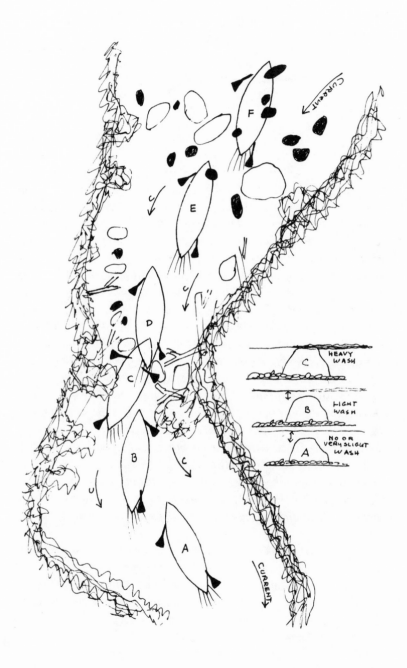

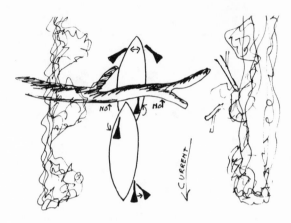

We are back to the overhang where many of the same rules from page 125 apply. Bend down, way down, even get down on your knees if necessary to go through. If the canoe bow will make it under, you will too if you are low enough, but one at a time. As you approach, have sufficient headway with the canoe to be able to slide through with a minimum of paddling. As the bowman approaches the overhang, he boats his paddle. It is now up to the sternman to exert enough power to go through easily. He does this by paddling forward and correcting if necessary in order to head the canoe right into the current and not risk being swept off course. If he lets the canoe go to the right or left, you will not make it. Once committed, he has to pinpoint the passage and go for it. As the bowman gets down with the overhang behind him, the sternman gives the okay and the bowman quickly gets back into paddling position. By paddling on both sides as quickly as possible he maintains canoe headway and straight ahead direction. The stern paddler boats his paddle and ducks down, and the canoe is pulled through by the bow paddler. Once through, alternate paddle while you look at the next project.

This kind of problem can be complicated by rocks and snags that intensify the need to know your path ahead of time and to stick with it. This is a true billiard shot and you must knock the ball in the pocket. Situations like this accentuate the need for very accurate canoe control and paddle savvy—the art of canoeing at its best. Trials like this will hone your senses.

6

Trip Six—Fast Narrow River Downstream

For the sake of continuity, we will create a fast and narrow stream with basically the same problems as you experienced in the slower river. You will note that all decisions will have to be made quicker, more precisely, and usually with a bit more strength and commitment. This time, the river is traveling merrily downstream at from 5 to 10 miles an hour, and it is a bit narrower than our first water. With more experience it will seem a bit wider and less threatening than before. Here you will feel the current acting on your canoe much more forcefully, and as it does, your reaction should be in kind. As in all downstream running, the canoe is much more at the mercy of the current than it is when you are paddling upstream; try to over correct and over paddle to work your changes to the extreme. It is better to have a comfortable margin than just barely make it through. Remember that we are preparing you for the ultimate—white water canoeing. You will not find it difficult if you can survive this river both up and down.

So let's go. Both paddlers are ready, alert. This should be fun.

Starting at A, *we see a lot of fast water ahead—not white water with surf, but plenty fast with twisting currents. Since we can't see much margin for our track through the maze, we should look it over in advance. The first part of the curve at* C *is pretty easy, but a sharp turn is required from there down and around to the end of the run. Remember that this water is running from five to seven miles an hour, fairly fast. Quick currents can jump it to ten miles per hour; you will have to make some quick paddle switches and react instantly since the canoe will begin to look too large for the trail you have selected.*

At A, *both are paddling on the right side, heading under the tree on the left; a stern correction points the bow out immediately to skirt the rocks. Stay away from the right side. If you were to go right, it would be hard to make the next turn.* C *finds you heading for the left side of the bend while the current tries to whip your stern around. This time you let it. With both paddling on the right side, make the power stroke straight through to* E *and fend off as you go through, switching paddle positions if necessary. As the bow comes to just behind* F, *do a fast paddle switch. Edge around to position for* G. *By correcting and switching, the stern paddler puts the canoe in the clear. This is all fast work, requiring both paddlers to keep in touch, verbally. This kind of a run in a larger river would be just the same. Look at the diagram, imagine the canoe about half size, and run through it again. To have fun with it, speed up the water!*

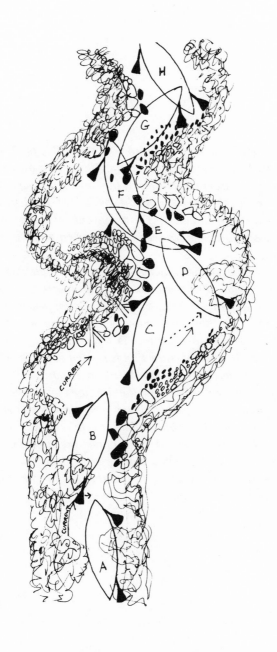

It takes a little looking ahead to spot the visible boulders in this open water run. Avoid rocks with only the tip exposed or sunken ones that will cause current ripples if they are high enough. The basic current here is right down the middle, but it is twisted here and there by the clusters of boulders. Those currents can slip your canoe around. Keep your paddles deep for sudden corrections, both bow and stern.

At A, the bow paddler switches from right to left in order to bring the canoe around. The stern paddler helps, correcting to slide by B, and then suddenly switches and corrects to immediately point the bow for the C position. After moving about three feet, the reverse correction is needed to swing into D. The current will be an aid in swinging the stern; stern correction is needed at E as the bow paddler guards the left bow. Both paddlers are in harmony at F to face what is coming next. Note how the decisions and directions must happen by anticipation. There is no hurry, however. Let the river slip by under you. Use your paddles to hold back when you are unsure how to make the next turn. Widen the stream a bit, strike up a faster current, and you are in for a real trip. There are many rivers like this all over the nation, and they are fun when both paddlers begin to think as one.

This stream is wider but beset by many boulders and shallows in a difficult maze. First study the current and note the heaviest flow. Do not be misled by wave wakes behind boulders into thinking this is the current. The best water will be rather smooth, but even flowing. Note the water ahead at C, D and E, for that is the tough part of this one. The turn from B to C must be made quickly.

So, beginning at A, with alternate side paddling, point the bow toward B; as soon as you reach B, make a very fast turn to the left with the bow paddler switching and the stern paddler correcting. The current will slip you to D with a little forward motion to slide through the hole; when you are about halfway through, make a fast right angle switch in order to find the path down to E. There, a fast turn puts you under the tree and to the side of the rock — you are home free. This whole run is made in a minute or two if you take it slow. In high water, this river will give you a bit more range above the underwater rocks, but the problem is the same; the faster current flow will necessitate faster and more pronounced action with the paddles.

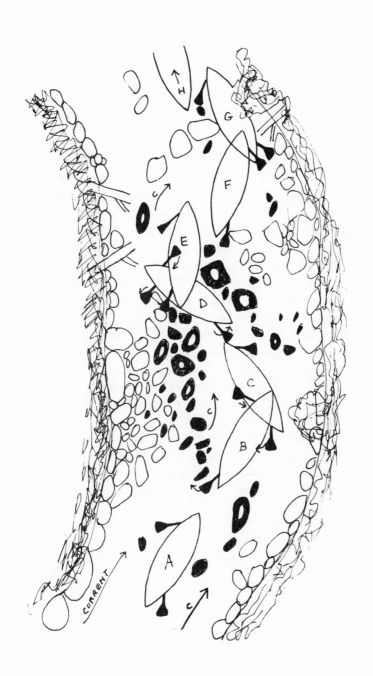

This is a wider river but it looks like a giant jigsaw puzzle with all those rocks, current rips, and dry gravel bars. At X is a point of decision. You could go to the right but the shallows are questionable. At a higher water level this might be the better way to go, but not now. Stick to the heavy water to the left even though the passage is narrow. This is fast water now — about ten miles an hour — but has only ripples, not white stuff yet. Look it over carefully when you are out there and mentally search for the way through. From A, with alternate paddling, it will be wise for the bow paddler to stay on the left side and watch ahead for rocks underwater (not shown). At the Question Mark, you have already decided to go to the left. At C, the stern paddler corrects slightly to point the bow between the rocks. A little more pressure by the bowman puts the bow in correct aim at D. As the current swings the canoe to the right, the bowman switches to the right for a quick paddle to keep away from the shallows. F puts you in the clear for the next run.

This is beautiful water. When you are both in tune, it can be a delight to figure the angles almost automatically. Make the choices and then gently but firmly allow the current to do most of the work for you.

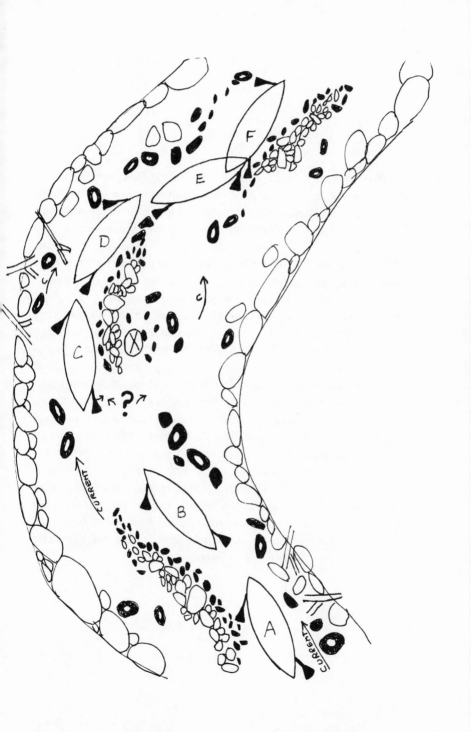

Here we have a beautiful slalom course. It looks hard and it is. But many rivers contain such stretches that make you appreciate the slow and long lakelike stretches. Sharp anticipation is needed here for accuracy. The current doesn't tell you very much since it is so broken up. An obvious course is impossible to see at first. Pick your way on this one, holding back constantly; but in an instant, you must make strong and direct strokes quickly so that the canoe will react accordingly. There are no shoreline problems, so let's take it from A, with both paddling on the right side. As the canoe approaches B, the stern paddler almost stops the canoe as the bow paddler switches to the left side. A possible way would be toward X, but careful scrutiny will tell you that is not the way through. As the canoe slides through B the stern paddler corrects sharply; the bowman paddles hard to point the canoe to the right heading to D. In a split second both bow and stern paddlers have to make a right angle by correcting and alternate paddling. As the canoe drifts down toward F, it is pointed to the rocks ahead, and you will be within inches of that snag. Correct instantly with a sharp right as the canoe heads toward the rock below. Correct again to H and it is all over. With luck, you still have paint on the canoe sides. If you try this kind of stretch in higher water with more speed from the current, you will really have a slalom course. Notice how delicate and responsive your canoe is. Nothing boring here.

A look over this water will reveal what cannot be shown in the diagram. The first part of the run, at C, is actually a vortex of current formed by a kind of V configuration of the rocks leading to a point at the end of B. A current vortex also comes to a point at I. The layout at G is partially this kind of water but with plenty of space to the left. The first section, complete with its nasty kind of bend, really causes the current to whisk through there; watch the drift of the canoe as you leave A and proceed with a correction at B, more correction at C, and paddle switching at D. Slow down and angle sharply to F being careful not to bump that rock on the right side. Ease the canoe forward for a fast correction to G. H and I are pretty easy until you are faced with that big rock straight ahead. Which side? Well, look ahead. What's there in front of you?

After handling the preceding runs with reasonable accuracy and no problems other than sudden frights, you will have become pretty good at downstream fast water. We'll take you upstream through the same stretches — and by that time you can write a book. One good way to practice these sudden changes and switches is to take the canoe out on flat water and go through an imaginary slalom run, or arbitrarily see how close you can come to docks, markers, snags, rocks, or other craft that have been advised of your actions. Both paddlers will get to know each other by telepathy. May your runs be smooth.

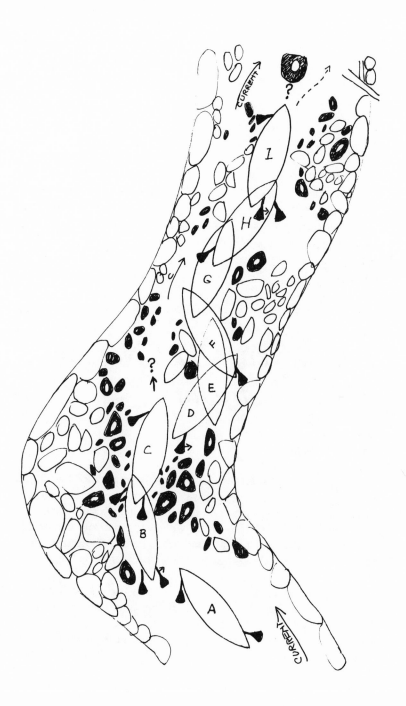

7

Trip Seven — Fast Narrow River Upstream

Quite a bit different than the slower river, wasn't it? Rest a bit and we'll return to base, working our way upstream over the same water. Again, note that you are much more in the driver's seat when paddling upstream, though the current will try to twist your course and to swing the canoe out from under you. There is no need to hurry upstream, so take it slow — not easy, but slow — and you'll make out okay.

The single paddler had best kneel for this trip. He will have to act as both stern and bow paddler at the same time to make his corrections and point his way into the currents.

In a sense this faster water can be easier to handle since it is usually better defined — the problems and choices more easily handled. This kind of water is very common over most of the hilly and mountainous country. It has many variables during the season of spring high water — mid-season medium water and late-season low water.

Learn all these moods and be ready for anything. A sudden storm well upstream can suddenly raise the water and you have to be ready.

We are going over familiar waters upstream. It will be a lot easier than it was going down, but you are going to have to contend with the vagaries of the current which will wobble your canoe course and flip your stern around. The current will also work on your bow as you head into it, trying to tilt you off course. This requires a lot of correcting by the sternman to keep the nose in the right direction and a lot of paddle shifting by both paddlers. Since the current is running about five miles an hour—a hefty current to buck—you won't be breaking any records. At A, the current will try to drive your stern to the left; so the sternman corrects as he enters between the rocks and approaches B. Neither changes paddle positions even at C, where a turn to maneuver the canoe between the rocks at D is proposed. E finds you well under control and abreast of the rocks there. It looks simple and it is—that is, if you have looked ahead carefully to pick your path among the rocks. When you get out on that water, you will see the current ripples and will be able to judge where to head and how to get there. One thing about upstream paddling: since you move slowly and are under better control all of the time, it is merely a matter of skill and a little correcting to put you on course and keep you there.

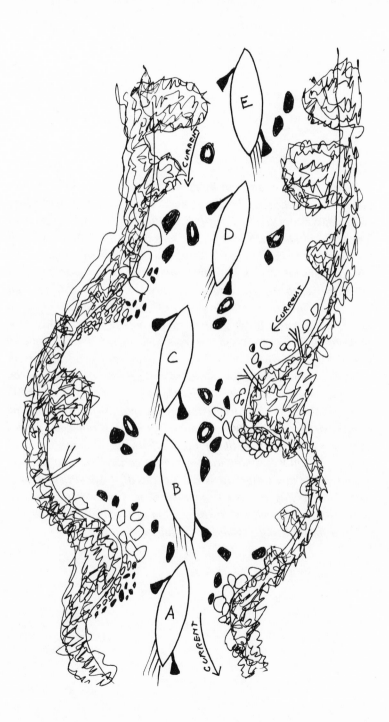

Familiar water again, but it presents an almost new set of conditions when you are paddling upstream. There are lots of rocks here and shallows that can be identified. At A, look carefully at the pattern you will construct and follow as you move up. Since the current wants to swing you to the right, you need to correct a little here as you head to B. There, both are paddling on the same side in order to swing over to the left toward C. Allow the current to swing you, but not too far into that shoreline. At C, the bow paddler shifts to the right side preparing to go through the narrow space between the rocks at D. The canoe swings immediately to the right as the current wafts you around at E. The bow paddler, seeing the narrow space between those rocks, switches paddle positions causing you to shoot right through. Again, this is easier than going downstream here, and, since you are proceeding slowly into the fast current, you don't have to make any split second decisions. It is fun water as well as very good fishing water of the kind found on many northern streams. It could be poled too — a subject coming up a bit later. In exceptionally low water, this stretch could offer some pesky problems. Imagine this stretch with a lot more rocks and with those underwater rocks visible all across the bottom of the stretch. Facing into the sun on that setup would keep you squinting.

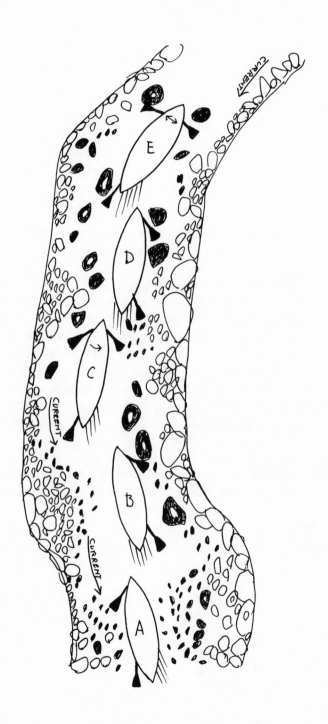

This is a bit wider section, but there are a few quick turns to make as you survey the layout of rocks and snags ahead of you. Pause at A *and see the moves you will have to make right away. A look farther down shows an easy path through. Make sure you scrutinize that bottom, however. There are a lot of rocks along that gravelly bottom that are not shown. At a lower water stage, the infringement from both sides of the stream will increase, narrowing the current into a faster rush and shallowing the whole course. At* A, *right under that overhanging tree, a paddle switch and some force puts you on the correct angle for* B. *Slide between the rocks with the stern paddler switching. Correct to point the bow to the left into the opening.* D *is a cinch as you head straight up and away with a slight bend at* E.

This is a good stretch to test your subtle correcting and bow angling. Both sternman and bowman can do a little angling exercise here, swinging from left to right and back again, just for practice.

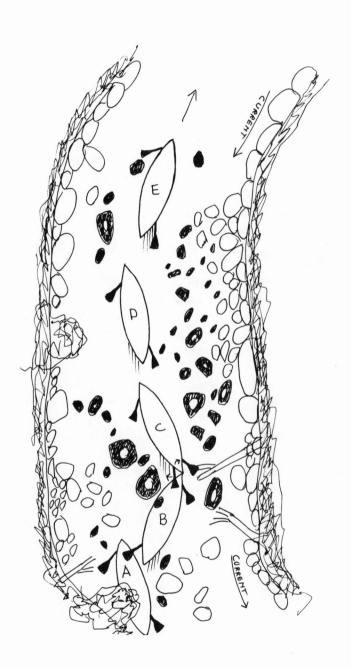

Here is your chance to pause a moment to survey the bend in the river and note the gravel bars, big center-current boulders, and the whims of the current as it winds through the maze. There are not many problems from shoreline snags. There is one section at the Question Mark where you might be a bit confused. To the left side it looks shallow with a couple of big boulders showing. The right side looks quite fast and would require more paddling power and accuracy since this is a current sluiceway; all the way through very accurate and controlled paddling is necessary to negotiate it.

At A, you maneuver between the large rock and the gravel bar where the current is really whizzing by. Without switching positions you ease to B, watching your stern as it tends to slip in the direction of those rocks. At C, you are facing a narrows and again face a surge of current, necessitating accurate and powerful control of the bow. With a slight turn to the left leading to D, you continue down the narrow corridor to the bend at E with the bowman switching sides to the left. At F, it is just a matter of paddling the canoe right through.

Low water here would offer some problems; in extremely dry conditions it might necessitate your walking the canoe through the shallows. High water, on the other hand, would not alter your course; but it would make it quite a bit harder to control the canoe while moving forward at a decent speed.

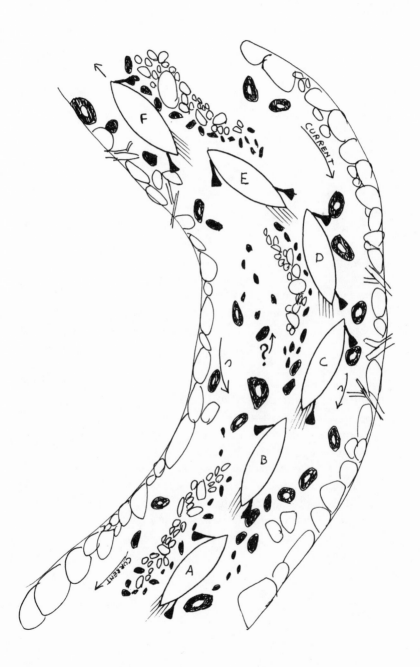

Here we have a snaky type of course to follow once we can make it out and plan it. From A, it looks as though there are a lot of options, but there are really not that many when you have a keen eye. Looking at it here (from above) is one thing, but just for the exercise, raise the book up and flatten it out to approximate the view of the actual stream as you would see it from the canoe height. Looks a bit complicated, doesn't it? Look closer, at least for the first part of the stretch. Since you are not being carried downstream by the current and thus can make your own speed against the current, there is no hurry. You can take it section by section and figure out the moves at close distances. At A, then, you will travel between the rocks and the gravel with a bowman paddle switch to fend off that snag as the sternman corrects so that the canoe heads to the right. Due to the action of the current, the sternman will switch to the left and correct quickly to swing the bow to C. He swings back again to the right side to proceed to D, right near a big rock which the bowman can handle. E is a slight swing to the right with both paddling on the right side to offset the current and point the canoe in to the left towards F. The bow paddler switches to the left at F, and the stern paddler corrects to point the canoe to G. Wow, that was fun, swinging back and forth and slipping right over all that current. A canoe goes over it all; a rowboat has to mush through it. Your canoe almost flies. The delicacy needed is a pleasure to deal out over that everchanging water.

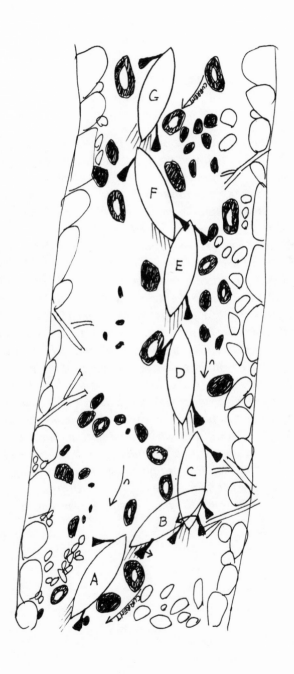

You made the right decision to put that rock to your right as you enter this run. You followed the deepest and heaviest water, and that is a good rule to follow. There could be complications that you couldn't see in the rocks to the right side. At A, the bow paddler, switching to the right side to aid in the battle with the current, points the canoe to B; you are headed right for the rocks upstream. The stern paddler is alert to the need for a correction to slide by the rocks at C and then for a correction and paddle switch to the left side. The bow paddler switches to the left side as you come to D. The stern paddler switches to the right and corrects quickly toward E. You are away free at F to look at what's ahead.

This all looks easy on the diagram as seen from above. Raise the picture to almost eye level and see how complicated it would look if you were actually in the canoe. A great many of the larger streams and rivers contain water like this, and it is a delight to find your way around. Again, you are not at the mercy of the current. You can go through it as fast as you want and can allow the current to help you in many cases. You will learn subtle canoe movement working with the current. After a few runs you will note how little you have to do other than forward paddling to gain speed against the current. In low water, this stretch could be a real drag; at high water it could be a really tough assignment requiring constant and powerful strokes to make it through.

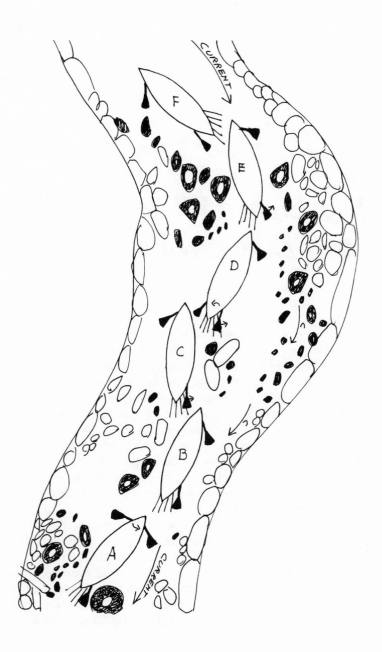

8

Trip Eight—White Water Runs Downstream

Where there is white water—that is, water that is flowing fast over obstructions such as mini-falls, rocks and gravel—you will find a myriad of conditions. There may be deep holes, back eddies, whirlpools, erratic currents, strong swings of heavy water, and bland, flat, quiet stretches. Many rivers and large streams have these water types but they also have relaxing moments when you will encounter long straight stretches. Your only concerns will be sticking to the main current if you are going through or diverting to the shallower slow water to light a cigarette, fish, or take a photograph.

You will use your paddle for paddling; but in some cases you will use it as a rod to pry the canoe away from passing rock or gravel cluster or even a sunken log.

Basically, the water is similar to what you have traveled so far. The pace, however, is upped and your errors in decisions will show up quicker as you descend. The reaction of your canoe will be much more pronounced. Very fast and sometimes strong paddling action will require faster and better timing between the sternman and the bowman. Switching will be quicker and you will have to get that paddle deeper in the water, know what kind of stroke is needed, and make it in a pronounced way.

This is really fun. The water is not dangerous if you don't try to take it too fast; learn to hold back or at least slow down a bit, not allowing the current to take you at its pace.

Enough advice. Let's go.

Six Classes of White Water Runs
American Canoe Association

1. Occasional small rapids with low regular waves not over one foot high. Course easily determined. Rescue spots all along. Shallow.
2. More frequent rapids. Eddies and whirlpools offer no trouble. Ledges not over three feet high with a direct uncomplicated chute. Course easily determined. Waves up to three feet high but avoidable. Water more than three feet deep.
3. Long rapids, maneuvering required. Course not easily recognizable. Waves up to five feet high, mostly regular, avoidable. Strong cross currents. Good rescue spot after each rapid.
4. Long rapids, intricate maneuvering. Course hard to determine, waves high (up to five feet), irregular, avoidable or medium (up to three feet) and unavoidable. Strong cross currents, eddies.
5. Long continuous rapids, tortuous; require frequent scouting. Extremely complex course. Waves large, irregular, unavoidable. Large scale eddies and cross currents. Rescue spots few and far off. Special equipment: decking, life jackets.
6. Long continuous rapids without letup. Very tortuous; always scout. Waves very high (above five feet), irregular, unavoidable. Powerful cross currents. Special equipment. Limit of canoeability, involves risk of life.

Before you canoe a questionable stretch of water, go ashore well ahead of white water sections to make decisions whether to run, portage, or line it out. While ashore, mark theoretical moves through rocks, snags, and tricky currents. Know what you are getting into and whether you should or not.

Every expert has been doused and capsized—that's the way to perfection. Leave all gear and duffle ashore and wear life jackets and helmets. Don't be scared . . . it's fun! All aboard.

Before you start on this first white water run, better take a good look and find the course. This is very fast water and there are a lot of rocks and pesky currents to contend with. While the path looks obvious on the diagram, in real life it is not. Scan that water, rock by rock, current by current, noting the heavy water which will hold your canoe and the ultra white that will possibly have bad rocks that you cannot see underneath. On this run, you should both try and hold as you go down through. Make sure you both know where the path is and agree on paddle switching and fending off the rocks as you go by them. Your canoe is going to be seriously affected by the currents. But remember that washes behind or below rocks are much slower than the uninterrupted current; take advantage of washes, even though they are likely to be shallow.

At A, there is a narrow passage. Toward B, you both switch as the current buffets your direction. At C, the current is really on your tail, so a paddle switch is needed to proceed to D. You literally slide to E through that narrow passage. Handle the shallow but fast flue of current at F very carefully, holding the stern from swaying back and forth.

If you do not hit anything, this run should take only about thirty seconds. But it can be taken much slower, and beginners should hold back at all the "canoe letters" without allowing the canoe to swing to the sides. In many cases, you can use rocks to help you in your direction and control.

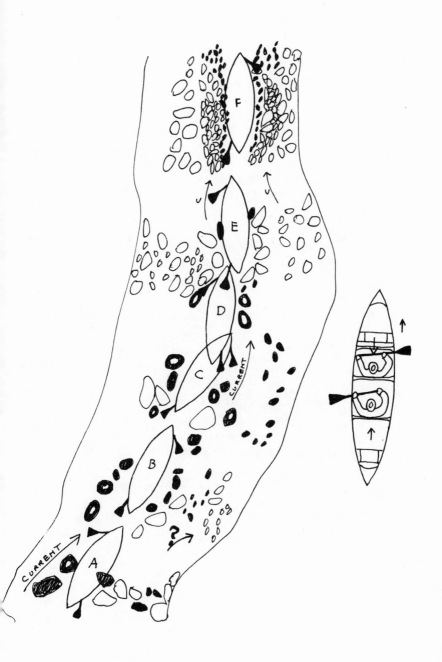

This is a bit wider river but a fast one nonetheless. At first, it appears to be a maze of big boulders. Study the current as it sways back and forth behind rocks in the washes and note the generally dark water. These stretches are deep enough to require contemplation before you enter. The most important thing to do is to plot the course ahead of time since there are no options in this run. Take it slowly as you go down. The margins are slim, and you both will have to use your paddles to fend off the rocks as you go through each turn.

While alternate side paddling at A, you can see ahead to B. You can also see the need for a quick turn into position C. The bow paddler switches to the right side and into D. You are both paddling on the right. As the canoe is swept toward the rocks at E, you hold and ease through there with an anticipated left angle turn into F in order to handle that shallows at G and through it to H. Note that on all such runs you will both have to switch paddles constantly, letting each other know by orders or obvious moves. This is a particularly nasty run, even though on the diagram it looks fairly easy. (We don't show the currents and their effects on your canoe.) Again, take it easy. Back paddle to help slow, or even stop, your forward motion until you are absolutely sure where you are going and how.

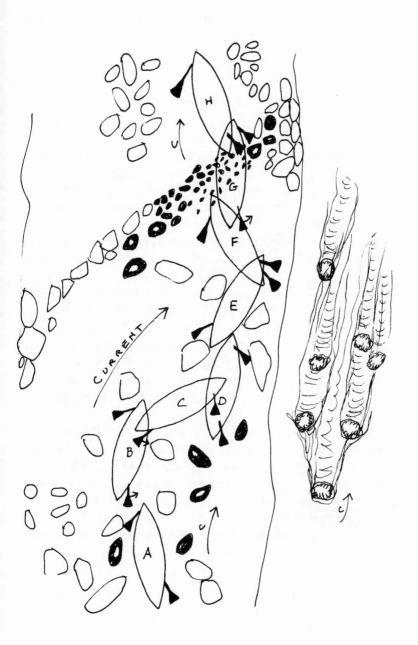

This is a wide stream which is rushing down in mixed water and deeper currents. Those boulders are big and there are lots of hidden ones. Since you could be faced here with a couple of alternate routes, you should do a little studying. The first Question Mark above B is the first alternative; you could follow it rather than go to the right. But you can't measure that depth and those rocks accurately. Since the CDE course shows more even flowing water, that is the best path to follow. In higher water levels, the left route might be easier to handle because it would be slower. At B now, after drifting from A, both paddlers are working the left side of the canoe to make an easy turn at C where the canoe is almost across the current. It is a difficult time to keep the canoe upright and moving in the direction shown. This calls for strong paddling and a sudden stop to make the turn to D. This is one of the most difficult tricks to perform in fast water, as is the turn to D where the current is arguing with you. E is merely the extension of the efforts at D. But there is an anticipated turn and a fend off at F; the current whips the stern to the left and you glide smoothly down to G. Study this one again and visualize the current washes and the pressures you will be working it with. Work with the water, not against it. A long log would make it through there with little trouble, just flowing down naturally; but the log, not floating as you are, would not be affected by the surface currents. Mind your tail in this one and keep the bowman advised about switching and about the direction you have chosen.

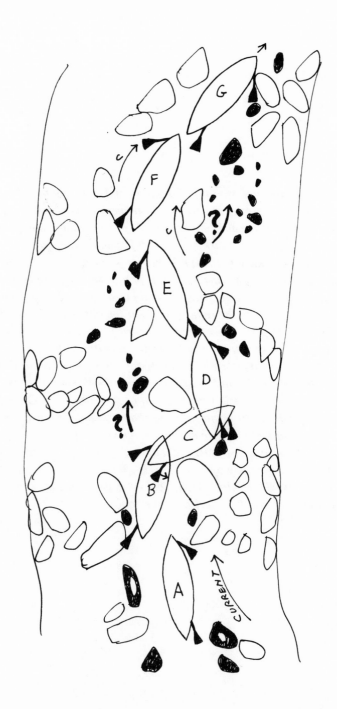

This is a mixture of gravelly shallows and some big boulders. As you study the layout, you will find the main current you must use after looking at the alternate routes. At A, you could take the right lane in the Question Mark area, but it is shallow and questionable. Might be the best way though in higher water levels. From A to B is a mere drift on the current, but it points you to those two rocks at the right of C. Anticipate this and cut in as close as possible to the sunken rocks to the right of C, even fending off before making a fast turn into D. The current will turn your tail to the right, so watch it because you have to skirt that long line of boulders ahead of D on the right. Position yourself for the narrow run to E. The twist to F is needed quickly as the current will tend to throw you into the rocks at the left bank. As your bow heads for G, make a slight switch heading you into the shallows and very white water through that section, perhaps with some very fast paddle shifting. Correcting in such fast water is not always effective, and paddle shifts must be made quickly by both. This is a tricky fast section, so study it a bit, visualizing the currents below those rocks, as well as the main current and its effect on your canoe.

This is typical of a smaller stream at low water, or at least medium low water, where a great many big rocks are bare. The curve of the river tells you that the main current is strong in its ability to sway your stern as you go through. All of this water is white or semi-white with no lapses into dark and slower water. Almost every rock in the picture throws a fast and white wake, hiding many of the underwater rocks. We have only one alternate route at the Question Mark; but even though that water looks as though it might not be as fast, that is the bow in the bend of the river. It is fast and loaded with side stream snags that you will have to avoid as you slip through on your fast run. So stick to the center run.

Starting at A, as you glide through the narrows, the current is going to pressure you to the left. At B, the stern paddler is really digging to aim you to C where the paddler has to fend off that rock on the right side. The drift to C must be aimed perfectly. At the same time, the stern paddler has to steer toward a turned position at D, with a wide sweep of his paddle to make it around. The bow paddler fends off the snag and helps turn the canoe to position E, switching fast to contend with the position you want to turn at F. Quite a run for you. Lots of fun, but remember to slow down, even stop if necessary, by holding onto rocks or digging the paddle into the gravel. No need to go for broke and wonder. Wondering will skin the paint off the canoe.

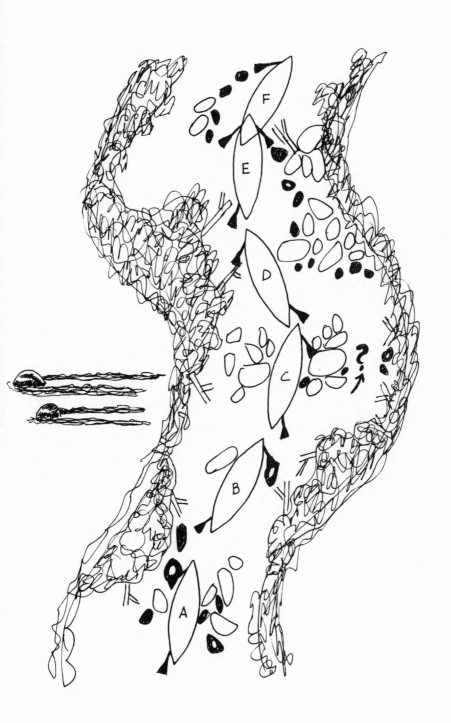

Here we have an almost hairpin turn with a lot of shallows, half hidden boulders and many snags along the route, plus an overhang. Now that is quite a project to entertain from your position at A. As you did while flowing with the slow river downstream stretch, you try to keep the bow pointed toward the lily pads, for this is relatively quiet water. That stream bend to the right is a frantic mess of half-hidden boulders and snags to be avoided. Watch the current and its pressure to swing your stern right into it. At B, you could decide to go to the right following the deepest and fastest current. But it is fraught with dangers ahead in that cluster of underwater rocks which doesn't really show you just how deep the water is through there. So keep to the left in the bend to D, holding the stern away from the drift to those rocks and the snag on the left. Now, at E, you are heading to pass under that overhang. Since in fast water this is quite a trick, you will be glad you have rehearsed it in slower water before. Ready, get set, duck, and go! and when you rise up you have the alternative of going to the left or right of those two half-submerged rocks. Take the shallow route by the lily pads, and at H you are in the clear. Like all of this white and semi-white water, this is a fast stretch which you can delay by holding back when necessary. Always look ahead, and be audible with your commands as you move through. After a few runs like this, you will become more and more competent. You will begin to think "together," react instantly, and have fun.

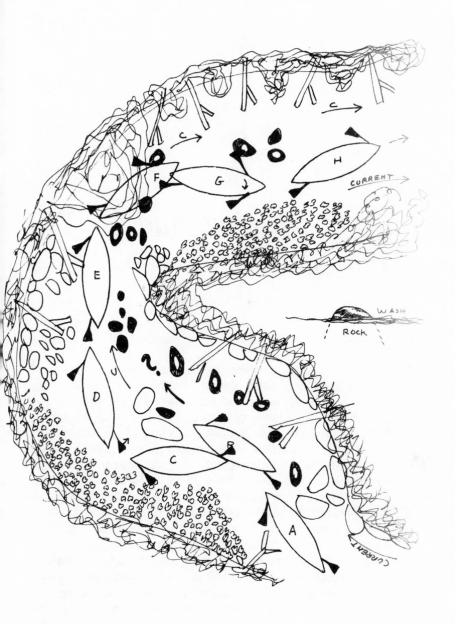

9

Poling, Lining, and Portaging

POLING

Well, we made it to our point of turning around. But there is another lesson to work on, and that is poling. The stretch ahead is of medium speed, not too curvy and quite shallow, so it will serve as a good workout. You could have poled and paddled the stretch we have just worked, but let's just take a little of this water in order to get used to the poling sequences and the right way to stand up in a moving canoe. The bow paddler will stay down in place and aid when necessary as a speed-controlling power. He will also act to help turn the canoe when necessary to avoid a rock or gravel bar and generally steer the course since he is up front.

In the stern, you will be able to see into the water to watch for underwater logs, rocks, and other hazards that the bowman might miss. You will also be better able to judge the currents and select which currents or direction to follow within a given current as it carries you downstream. You control the pace aided by the bow paddler.

To stand in the canoe, you take the pole in both hands and hold it across the canoe, parallel to the water. You don't put it in or even drag it in the water yet. You use it only when needed. Later it will be good to let it drag in the water and in the shallows over the gravel and rocks. Since it is a good way to contact the bottom, let it act as a sort of drag when needed.

Stand up now with your feet firmly braced against the canoe bottom. Holding the pole sideways, move it around for balance and feel. As you drift down an easy run, work your body a bit to note how the canoe balance reacts to each movement. Keep knees slightly bent for "spring." Swing the pole around and rotate your body from the waist, back and forth, in order to feel the extent you will need to pivot in this way to pole and to balance the canoe. The bow paddler can help in balancing, but not much.

Now, that was not as difficult as it looked. In a couple of instances, when you bumped into rocks or gravel bars, the action almost threw you; be prepared to compensate using your legs and body as a shock absorber. When negotiating a tricky situation, don't stand stiff legged. Bend your knees and even lean forward a bit from the belt. When you have stopped the canoe, placed your pole upstream of you, and pushed off into the current, keep your balance. The canoe just might take off more quickly than you thought it would if the bow paddler was caught unaware or didn't realize he should slow down a bit.

Poling Upstream

As you learned in previous waters, it is easier to proceed upstream since you have control of your pace. Because the canoe knifes through the current, your direction can be more accurate and definitive. The bow paddler now really works for his living, paddling upstream to aid in the poling. He has to switch more often than he did going downstream. He will need to keep an eye out for underwater rocks that might not be as easily seen on the way up and use his paddle to fend the canoe away from trouble. He must study the wave and wash behind obstructions; he can and must guide you now more than before. In many cases you merely hold what he has gained by forward paddling. Cooperation is needed here, and it is best to take directions from the bowman since he has to fend off the bow and keep the course in line.

When trying to go through water that is too shallow for paddling

Poling is very similar to paddling as far as finding the way through a rocky situation. It is similar, too, in planning for current effects on the canoe as you go down through a given run. In many of the previous trips, both paddlers learned to slow the canoe down and even use the paddle to hold tight on the bottom. Poling is just an extension of this. The pole merely replaces the paddle because it is next to impossible to paddle through some stretches of river. The bow paddler can aid in directing the canoe and paddle or scuff the bottom to help the sternman who is doing the poling. This combination is used on many northern rivers and streams that are shallow, fast and rocky. Fishing guides generally pole rather than paddle their bow passenger and prefer that he keep his paddle out of the water. An experienced paddler hardly needs a bowman at all. He can negotiate the water all by himself. He takes his time and takes it easy, holding the canoe back against the current and allowing it to drift down current only when that is what he wants. This way, he can go through narrow runs and avoid fast currents by taking a side of the stream route. If he is guiding a fisherman, he can allow lots of time for casting, placing the canoe in the right spots and angles for the best approaches.

As you can see, the path has been made obvious here. The center current is relatively rock free and has a gravel bottom with just enough water to float the canoe. The bow paddler alternates sides as does the stern poler.

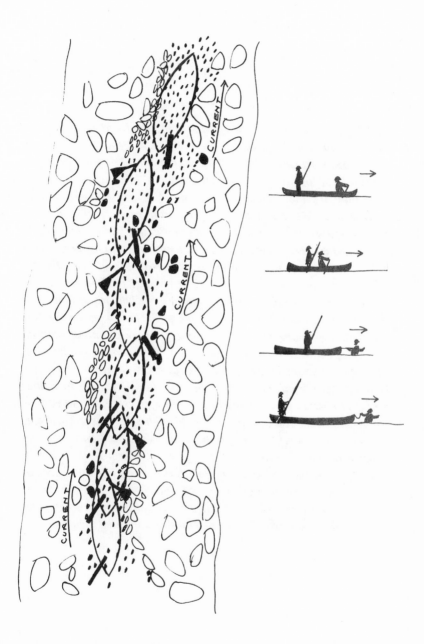

This is a boulder-strewn river with mud, sand and some gravel, and a lazy current to drift down on. Finding your way through and around the rocks and that one side stream overhang will not be as difficult as it looks if you take your time. While it is always best to try and find the route before you enter, it is almost impossible to do so here. Many decisions will have to be made a bit at a time.

At A, the main current is carrying you gently down. The sternman poles on the right side, the bowman on the left to fend off rocks and head the canoe toward B. There, it becomes a bit tight fitting between the obvious rocks and those underwater. The bowman keeps his paddle in the water as much as possible, reaching toward the bow quite often to fend off what lies ahead and also to keep an eye out so he can help to angle the bow. This calls for good communication to the sternman. In these tight situations, the bowman should take the initiative as far as steering and course direction is concerned. That fast turn from C to D is a case in point. The drift to E and the turn to F are to be handled slowly and with grace. G and H now become obvious. You inch the canoe through all of this to I and are free. In each case there have to be some very quick and accurate measurements and motions. Picking your way through this maze is quite a test of the experience gained in the preceding situations. It all comes due here. Being able to pole and paddle through means that there is virtually no water course that you cannot successfully get through, if you look, see, make your decisions, and then proceed.

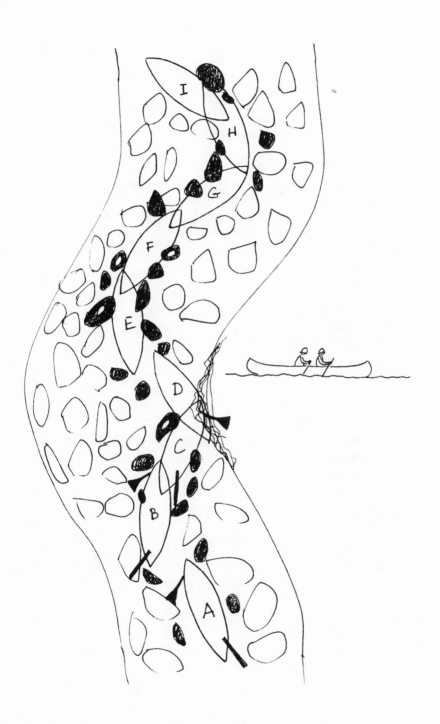

and combination paddling and poling, the next best procedure is to get out and walk. The bowman should get out first on this upstream run, and, taking the bowline in his hands, gently and slowly pick his way through the shallows; the sternman still stands up, poling the canoe to assist him. The canoe is much lighter now and the bow is up making it possible to drag the canoe over many of the shallows where it cannot float with two aboard.

Where you encounter very fast water that is impossible to paddle either up or down, shallows may offer the alternative course. Both can get out and walk, and, with two ropes, they can urge the canoe along the edge of the fast current, working it out from their path in the shallows. This is the preparation for lining.

LINING

This operation is somewhat complicated and requires some experience in order to handle the canoe in fast, choppy water where there are lots of tricky currents, large boulders and almost impossible conditions. The procedure calls for two lines of at least a hundred feet in length, but usually only about fifty to seventy-five feet are needed. The lines are attached to the canoe, and the canoe is slowly angled and allowed to follow in the current going downstream or to be pulled into the current on the upstream run past the tough area.

Lining is done as the last resort to portaging. It is the alternative when portaging is impossible because of swampy, brushy, or rocky conditions.

PORTAGING

Let's say you have been happily paddling downstream on a fast river and look ahead to see a maze of rocks and white water. If you are smart, you stop in your tracks to consider the next move and look for a safe way to canoe the water through the rough area.

At first glance it looks impossible to paddle through it. With valuable equipment aboard, cold water, and the danger of losing equipment in the fast water, you decide not to paddle through, or even try to pole through. If it is impossible to walk the canoe through, the only remaining alternative is portaging.

So, you both get out of the canoe for a look at the terrain and to investigate problems along the edge of the stream. You look for a suitable, walkable path around the white water where it will be the easiest to carry the canoe on your shoulders. You cut branches, if necessary, to make a part, though it is always recommended not to alter the natural conditions. Usually, on anything but a far out wilderness situation, someone has been there before you and a well worn path is obvious, though it might have grown over a bit since few travel that river.

With the path found and walked in a rehearsal, you go back to the canoe, unload all gear, and carry it to the exit point where you will reenter the river. The canoe is now lifted entirely on the shore before lifting it up on the shoulders of the one who lost the coin flip. Actually, if it is a short portage and over easy terrain, you can both lift the canoe by the ends or by the thwarts and merrily walk it along. But the actual portage routine should be mastered.

You can now understand and appreciate the tremendous advantages of owning a canoe and knowing how to use it for pleasures that no other craft can offer. It has taken you where no other craft can, and it has done it safely and quietly. The next step is to start in at the beginning of the book, shop around for a canoe and equipment, and take each step one at a time as we have presented it here. As you begin to follow these hints and directions, a great many more simplifications and alternatives will occur to you, and you will then be able to make every move count for pleasure and safety afloat. Like any other undertaking, it is always wise to think it out first and then act. By doing so, when an emergency arises, you will have already found the cure for the situation and can implement the needed motion to correct instantly.

Canoeing is not dangerous, any more than anything else is. You can drown from a boat as fast as you can from a canoe. You can upset any kind of craft, including a fifty-foot cruiser. You can crash a plane by simply not reading the problem correctly or not making a quick decision when needed.

Have fun, have relaxation, have recreation and sport. Your canoe will become a part of you. It will offer you a lifetime of contact with the water and an intimate feeling of oneness with all the nature around you if you command all of the equipment and that command

Lining. A *shows how to tie the lining rope to the forward and rear thwart, not the canoe seat. A canoe seat is not constructed to withstand this kind of pressure. Neither the anchor rope nor the towing rope should ever be tied to it.* B *shows the tie around the canoe bow to keep the line pressure low so as not to tip the canoe.*

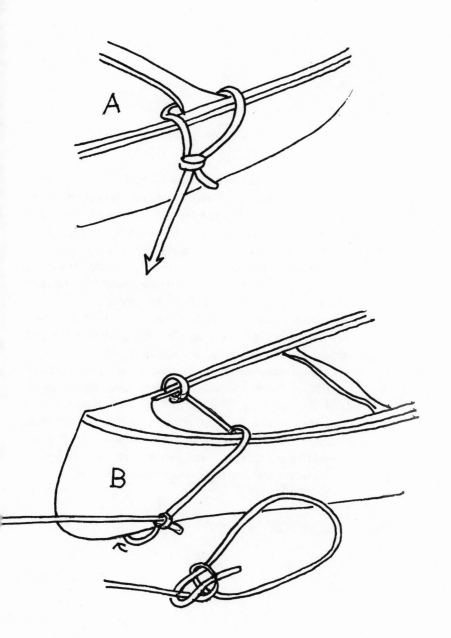

Lining (continued). With enough rope for both ties — generally at least a hundred feet is necessary — the two paddlers can ease the canoe along its course downstream, one steering it between any rocks that are about. It is a good idea also to keep the canoe to the side of the main current so it will not be pulled away from you or pulled against you too hard. You can control it easily; we suggest you try this several times in a practice run to become synchronized and to note how the canoe acts under such current stress.

Lining upstream is a bit more difficult since you will have to bring the canoe up against the current, all the while guiding it into and out of current and around rocks, and generally keep it under control. The upstream man controls the direction and the sternman keeps the stern of the canoe in line with the pressures so that the canoe proceeds as it is directed. The control for both upstream and downstream runs is made by pressure on the lines and lengthening or shortening the lines. If you follow through the sequence, you can see, by visualizing the current stress, just how to keep the bow in the proper direction and the stern under control as well.

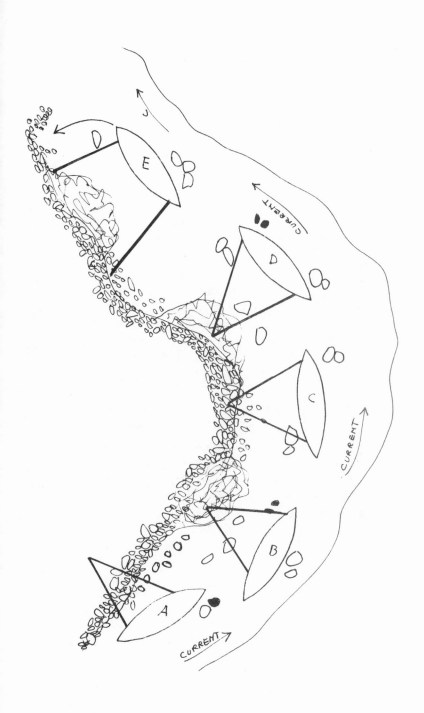

The first step in portaging the canoe is to empty it of all equip-ment and set it on the ground, open side up. Perhaps you have car-ried the canoe for short distances by grasping both gunwales, and, while bumping knees, you have been able to carry it sideways to or from the water rather than drag it.

The next step, before lifting it up for the portage stance, is again to grasp it by both thwarts a little ahead of center for lighter balance in the bow when you are carrying later. Neither hand will let go of the canoe from now on. At A, *you ease the canoe off the ground, and as you do you turn it sideways and allow the stern of the canoe to touch the ground behind you. This will act as a pivot later in the lifting and balancing unless you have another person around to balance it for you.* B *shows the completion of step one — getting the canoe upside down and balanced fairly well with both hands. It is very light now, since the weight is being pivoted by the stern. With yoke in place, you rest the thwart across the back of your shoulder about four inches below your neck. Adjust your neck to it and get into a comfortable position, allowing the canoe to rest there until you are well set for the lift off.*

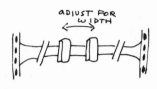

adjust for width

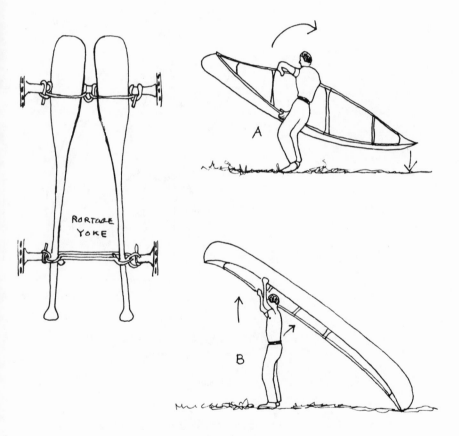

PORTAGE YOKE

A

B

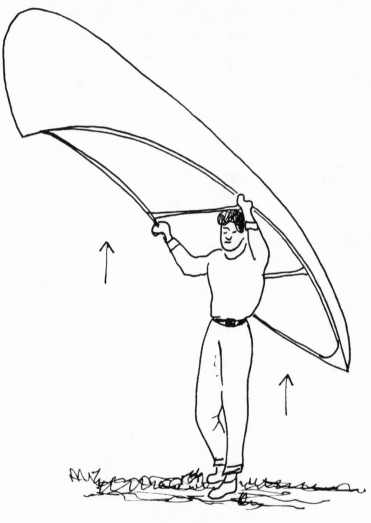

Portaging.

becomes second nature. Any new project is sometimes confusing and difficult and you are all thumbs. This will disappear in direct ratio to your attention and application to what we have outlined in these pages.

Appendix A

Canoe Manufacturers

Aladdin Products, Inc.
Dippa Ky-Nu Div.
Haskell Rd.
Westport Island, ME 04578
    1 model

Allagash Canoe
Francestown, NH 03043
    8 models

Alumacraft Boat Co.
315 W. St. Julien
St. Peter, MN 56082
    7 models

American Fiber-Lite, Inc.
P.O. Box 67
Marion, IL 62969
    5 models

Apple Line
146 Church St.
Amsterdam, NY 12010
    14 models

Badger Boat Builders
P.O. Box 97
Couderay, WI 54828
    2 models

Beaver Bark Canoes
R 3, Box 2
Woodruff, WI 54568
    1 model

Beaver Canoe Corp.
130 Orfuse Rd.
Toronto, ON
Canada M6A 1L9
    2 models

Blackhawk Canoe Co.
937 North Washington St.
Janesville, WI 53545
    1 model

Black River Canoes
Box 537
167 Railroad St.
LaGrange, OH 44050
    28 models

The Blue Hole Canoe Co.
Sunbright, TN 37872
    5 models

Bluewater Canoes
45 Speedvale Ave., E
Guelph, ON
Canada N1H 1J2
    11 models

Bluerock Woodcrafting
Box 138
Manitowish Waters, WI 54545
    3 models

Cal-Tek Engineering
29 Pemberton Rd.
Cochituate, MA 01778
    3 models

Cedarcraft Canoe
P.O. Box 1075
Osoyoos, BC
Canada V0H 1V0
    2 models

Cedar Creek Canoes
21 Edith La.
Wilton, CT 06897
    1 model

Cedarwood Canoes
385 Sunset Dr.
Fredericton, NB
Canada E3A 1B3
    9 models

Chicagoland Canoe Base
4019 N. Narragansett Ave.
Chicago, IL 60634
    7 models

Chief Manufacturing
737 Clearlake Rd.
Cocoa, FL 32922
6 models

CKC Products Co.
925 SE Clatsop
Portland, OR 97202
7 models

Coldwater Canoe Co.
P.O Box 324
Coldwater, ON
Canada L0K 1E0
1 model

Coleman Co.
250 N. St. Francis
Wichita, KS 67201
4 models

Core Craft, Inc.
P.O. Box 249, Ind. Park
Bemidji, MN 56601
13 models

Country Ways
15235 Minnetonka Blvd.
Minnetonka, MN 55343
4 models

Curtis Canoes
4587 Clay St.
Hemlock, NY 14466
3 models

Custom Canoes
R-1 West St. Rd.
Carthage, NY 13619
4 models

Dolphin Products, Inc.
142 Second St. W
Wabasha, MN 55981
8 models

Doug's Wood Products
3636 Edison Way
Fremont, CA 94538
4 models

Duck Trap Woodworking
P.O. Box 88, RFD 2
Cannan Rd.
Lincolnville Beach, ME 04849
3 models

Easy Rider Canoe &
Kayak Co.
P.O. Box 88108, Tukwila Br.
Seattle, WA 98188
28 models

Freedom Boat Works
Rte. 1, Box 12
North Freedom, WI 53951
3 models

Great Canadian
45 Water St.
Worcester, MA 01604
15 models

Grumman Boats
7 South St.
Marathon, NY 13803
16 models

Bart Hauthaway
640 Boston Post Rd.
Weston, MA 02193
5 models

Hoefgen Canoe Mfg.
SR 137, Hwy. M-35
Menominee, MI 49858
4 models

Indian River Canoe Mfg.
1525 Kings Ct.
Titusville, FL 32780
8 models

Island Falls Canoe Co.
RFD 3, Box 76
Dover-Foxcroft, ME 04426
5 models

Jensen Canoes
308–78th Avenue N
Minneapolis, MN 55444
9 models

J. W. Brown & Son
2684 Lake Winyah Rd.
Alpena, MI 49707
2 models

Kellogg & Miller Boat Works
146 Church St.
Amsterdam, NY 12010
12 models

Leavitt Quality Craft
R.F.D. # Box 1549
Hampden, ME 04444
3 models

Lincoln Canoes
Rt. 32
Waldboro, ME 04572
19 models

Lotus Canoes
7005 N. 40th St.
Tampa, FL 33604
4 models

Lowe Industries
P.O. Box 9891-44
Lebanon, MO 65536
4 models

Mad River Canoe, Inc.
P.O. Box 610
Waitsfield, VT 05673
29 models

Kevin Martin Boatbuilder
Box 441, RFD 1
Epping, NH 03042
4 models

Memphremagog Canoe
P.O. Box 466
Newport, VT 05855
2 models

Mentha Wooden Boat Co.
Rt. 2, 23rd St.
Gobles, MI 49055
5 models

Meyers Industries Ind.
P.O. Box E
Tecumseh, MI 49286
8 models

Michi-Craft Corp.
20000 19 Mile Rd.
Big Rapids, MI 49307
18 models

Mid-Canada Fiberglass Ltd.
Box 1599
New Liskeard, ON
Canada P0J 1P0
9 models

Millbrook Boats, Inc. —
John Berry
P.O. Box 14
Riparius, NY 12862
16 models

Misty River Marine Ltd.
#1 Third Ave.
Bluemenort, MB
Canada R0A 0C0
6 models

Mohawk Canoes
P.O. Box 668
Longwood, FL 32750
17 models

Moise Cadorette, Inc.
1710 Principale
St. Jean des Piles, PQ
Canada G0X 2V0
9 models

Morley Canoes
P.O. Box 147
Swan Lake, MT 59911
8 models

Noah Whitewater
Maple Springs Rd.
Box 193B
Bryson City, NC 28713
1 model

Nona Boats
1945-F Placentia Ave. ✓
Costa Mesa, CA 92627
6 models

Nova Craft Canoes
Glanworth, ON
Canada N0L 1L0
18 models

OAT Canoe Co.
RFD #1, Box 4100
Mt. Vernon, ME 04352
1 model

Old Town Canoe Co.
58 Middle St.
Old Town, ME 04468
18 models

Osagian Boats, Inc.
Hwy. 5 N., Box 213
Lebanon, MO 65536
7 models

Payne Canoes
2401 Virginia Dr.
Ottawa, ON
Canada K1H 6X2
6 models

Penrods' Canoe & River
Adventures
Box 93 RD #1
Summerhill, PA 15958
4 models

Pleasant Valley Canoe
151 Boston Rd.
Sutton, MA 01527
11 models

Perception, Inc.
P.O. Box 686
Liberty, SC 29657
2 models

Quintus Enterprises, Inc.
444 Lake Mary Rd.
Flagstaff, AZ 86001
7 models

Rainbow Boatworks
Box 159
Newport, VT 05855
19 models

Ranger Canoe Co.
Rte. 25, Tenny Mt. Hwy.
Plymouth, NH 03264
11 models

Rice Creek Boat Works
9715 Jackson St., NE
Blaine, MN 55434
2 models

Rivers & Gilman Moulded
Products, Inc.
Main Road, Box 206
Hampden, ME 04444
6 models

RKL Boatworks
Prett Marsh
Mt. Desert, ME 04660
3 models

Sawyer Canoe Co.
234 South State St.
Oscoda, MI 48750
12 models

Secret Harbor Boats
13700 Powerhouse Rd. ✓
Potter Valley, CA 95469
2 models

Seda Products
1085 Bay Blvd. ✓
Chula Vista, CA 92011
13 models

Shenandoah Canoe Co.
Rte. 3
Luray, VA 22835
2 models

Smoker-Craft
P.O. Box 65
New Paris, IN 46553
15 models

Stowe Canoes
Box 440
Braintree, MA 02184
9 models

Strongs Canoe Yard
Craftsbury Common
VT 05827
1 model

Sundance Canoe Co.
Box 1769, Hwy. 169
Graurnhurst, ON
Canada P0C 1G0
5 models

Supercedar Canoes
360 Sunnyside Ave.
Toronto, ON
Canada M6R 2R8
2 models

Tanana Canoes
2001 Old Greenboro Rd.
Jonesboro, AR 72401
4 models

Thomas J. Hill, Boatbuilder
Box 128
No. Ferrisburg, VT 05473
4 models

Tender Craft Boat Shop
67 Mowat Ave., #031
Toronto, ON
Canada M6K 3E3
3 models

Trailhead
1341-2 Wellington St.
Ottawa, ON
Canada K1Y 3B8
  2 models

Voyageur Canoe Co., Ltd.
Dept. 102
3 King St.
Millbrook, ON
Canada L0A 1G0
  21 models

Wabasca Canoe Co., Ltd.
General Delivery
Wabasca, AB
Canada T0G 2K0
  19 models

Wabash Valley Canoes
616 Lafayette Ave.
Crawfordsville, IN 47933
  18 models

Wellington Canoe
P.O. Box 466
Newport, VT 05855
  10 models

We.no.nah Canoes
P.O. Box 247
Winona, MN 55987
  31 models

Western Canoeing, Inc.
Box 115
Abbotsford, BC
Canada V2S 4N8
  27 models

White Canoe Co.
82 No. Brunswick St.
Old Town, ME 04468
  11 models

Willis Canoes
Curtis Rd., R.D. 3
Freeport, ME 04032
  1 model

Yukon Boat Works
1500 W. North Ave.
Milwaukee, WI 53205
  2 models

National Association of Canoe Liveries and Outfitters (NACLO)

ALASKA

Canoe Alaska
1738 Hilton Ave.
Fairbanks, AK 99701
(907) 456-8198
    Todd & Ron Davis
    Interior Alaska

R-L Enterprises
Box 86
Tok, AK 99780
(907) 883-4791
    Ron Liewer
    East interior rivers

ARKANSAS

Many Islands Camp
Rte. 2
Mammoth Springs, AR 72554
(501) 856-3451
    Woodrow Taylor
    Spring River

ARIZONA

Pack-n-Paddle Canoe Rentals
Old Western Trader
Topock Rte., Box 350
Topock, AZ 86436
(602) 768-4954
    Phil Villamoor
    Middle-Lower Colorado River

CALIFORNIA

Burke's Canoe Trips
P.O. Box 602, 8600 River Rd.
Forestville, CA 95436
(707) 887-1222
    Robert Burke
    Russian River

Cache Canyon River Trips
P.O. Box 34
Rumsey, CA 95679
(916) 796-3091
    Sam Fortner
    Cache Creek

California Rivers
21001 Geyserville Ave.
P.O. Box 468
Geyserville, CA 95441
(707) 857-3872
    Ann Dwyer
    Russian, Eel, Nararo, Rogue, Trinity

Canoe Trips West
2170 Redwood Hwy.
Greenbrae, CA 94904
(415) 461-1750
    Don Thoman

Cool River Rafts
3650 Lake Blvd.
Redding, CA 96003
(916) 275-8630
    Ken Edwards
    Sacramento River

Driftwood Resort
24630 Tehama-Vina Rd.
Los Molinos, CA 96055
(916) 384-2851
    Billy & Betty Timmons
    Sacramento River

Great Valley Canoe Trips
3213 Sierra Ave.
Riverbank, CA 95367
(209) 869-1235
Jim & Char Sughrue
Stanislaus, Merced,
Mokelumme, Tuolumne

National Outdoor College, Inc.
P.O. Box 962
Fair Oaks, CA 95628
(916) 338-3600
Ron Hilbert
American, Mokelumme,
Yube rivers

Pack-n-Paddle Canoe Rentals
LaVerne, CA
640 Arrow Hwy.
LaVerne, CA 91750
(714) 592-1986
Ernie Dioron
Owens, Kern, Colorado
rivers

Pack-n-Paddle Canoe Rentals
McIntyre Campground
Rte. 2, Box 179-D
Blythe, CA 92225
(714) 922-8205
Michael Wilson
Lower Colorado River

Pack-n-Paddle Canoe Rentals
The Outdoorsman
197 N. Main St.
Bishop, CA 93514
(714) 873-3015
Max Hernandez
Owens River, High Sierra
lakes

Paradise Ranch Rentals
P.O. Box 40
Klamath River, CA 96050
(916) 465-2251
Richard Tingley
Klamath River

Peter's Paradise Canoes
6303 Posey Lane
Paradise, CA 95969
(916) 877-8308
Mary & Virl Peters
Feather, Sacramento, Yuba

Trowbridge Recreation, Inc.
20 Healdsburg Ave.
Healdsburg, CA 95448
(707) 433-7247
Bill Trowbridge
American, Russian,
Colorado rivers

World of Whitewater
P.O. Box 708
Big Bar, CA 96010
(916) 623-6588 or 623-4456
O.K. & Glenna Goodwin
Klamath, Trinity, Hell's
Corner, Redwood,
Sacramento

Yu-Kan Canoe
2490 Henderson Rd.
Redding, CA 96002
(916) 243-9272
Tom, JoAnn & Neil Rucker
Sacramento River, Trinity,
Klamath

DELAWARE

Wilderness Canoe Trips, Inc.
Box 7125, Talleyville
Wilmington, DE 19803
(302) 654-2227
Jay Poole
Brandywine River

CONNECTICUT

River Running Expeditions,
Ltd.
Main Street
Falls Village, CT 06031
(203) 824-5579
Joan Manassee
Housatonic, Shepaug rivers

FLORIDA

AAA Canoes Rental & Sales
Rte. 2, Box 578
Cantonment, FL 32533
(904) 587-2366
Joe & Dee Riley
Perdida, Styx rivers

Adventures Unlimited, Inc.
P.O. Box 40
Bagdad, FL 32530
(904) 623-6197
Jack, & Esther Sanborn
Mike & Linda
Coldwater, Blackwater,
Juniper rivers

Adventures Unlimited Perdido
River
Rte. 4, Box 68
Cantonment, FL 32533
(904) 968-5529
David & Linda Venn
Perdido River

Alafia River Canoe Rentals
Rte. 1, Box 413-V
Valrico, FL 33594
(813) 689-8645
Bob & Sybil Cribbs
Alafia River

Alexander Springs Concessions
P.O. Box 112
Astor, FL 32002
(904) 759-2365
Roger G. Williams
Alexander Springs Creek

Bob's Canoes Rentals & Sales
Rte. 8, Box 34
Milton, FL 32570
(904) 623-5457
L. L. & Marie Plowman
Coldwater, Blackwater,
Sweetwater, Juniper

Canoe Outfitters of Florida
16346 106th Terrace N.
Jupiter, FL 33458
(305) 746-7053 and 747-1760
Eric & Sandy Bailey
Loxahatchee River

Canoe Outpost Arcadia
Rte. 7, Box 301
Arcadia, FL 33821
(813) 494-1215
Charlotte A. Bragg
Peace River

Canoe Outpost Little Manatee
18001 U.S. Hwy. 301 S.
Riverview, FL 33569
(813) 634-2228
  Chester & Faye Wood
  Little Manatee River

Canoe Outpost Lowry Park
P.O. Box 8323
Tampa, FL 33674
(813) 634-2228
  James Langford,
  Chester Wood
  Hillsborough River

Canoe Outpost Nobleton
P.O. Box 188, S.R. 476
Nobleton, FL 33554
(904) 796-4343
  George & Debby Blust
  Withlacoochee (South)

Canoe Outpost Oklawaha
Rte. 1, Box 1462
Fort McCoy, FL 32637
(904) 236-4606
  Robert & Bonnie Morrissey
  Oklawaha River

Canoe Outpost Suwannee
Rte. 1, Box 346
Live Oak, FL 32060
(904) 842-2192
  Suwannee, Alapaha,
  Withlacoochee rivers

Canoe Outpost Valrico
Rte. 1, Box 414K
Valrico, FL 33594
(813) 681-2666
  Rick & Charce Still
  Alafia River

The Canoe Shop
3102 S. Adams St.
Tallahasee, FL 32301
(904) 877-1792
  Sam Lamar
  150-mile radius

Estero River Canoe Livery
Rte. 1, Box 200 (U.S. 41)
Estero, FL 33928
(813) 992-4050
  Ron & Paula Stuller
  Estero River

Everglades Canoe
Outfitters, Inc.
39801 Ingraham Hwy.
Homestead, FL 33034
(305) 246-1530
  Chuck Harty, Sheri Leach
  Everglades

Hidden River Park Canoe
Livery
15295 E. Colonial Dr.
Orlando, FL 32817
(305) 568-5346
  Steve & Fran Hastings
  Econlockhatchee River

Juniper Springs Recreational
Service
Route 3, Box 651
Silver Springs, FL 32688
(904) 625-2808
  Harry & Shirley Fleury
  Juniper Springs Creek

Myakka River Outpost
2574 Parma St.
Sarasota, FL 33581
(813) 924-5895
  Norvia Behling
  Myakka River

Nature Trek, Inc.
Rte. 1, Box 1224
Palatka, FL 32077
(904) 328-4889
  Etoniah-Ocklawaha,
  Suwanee

GEORGIA

Ogeechee Canoe Outpost
213 San Fernando Blvd.
Savannah, GA 31406
(912) 925-9527
  John L. & Mary Alice
  Bittner
  Ogeechee, Savannah,
  Ohoopee, Canoochee

Raft, Georgia
P.O. Box 7363
Marietta, GA 30065
(404) 971-6553
  Robert A. Reichert
  N. GA waters,
  Chattahoochee River

ILLINOIS

Chicagoland Canoe Base, Inc.
4019 N. Narragansett Ave.
Chicago, IL 60634
(312) 777-1489
  Ralph Frese
  All Illinois waters

Fox Floats Raft Rental &
Canoe
Lincoln Ave &
Carpentersville Dam
Carpentersville, IL 60110
  Carol J. Schoengart
  Fox River

Reed's Canoe Trips
907 N. Indiana Ave., Rte. 50
Kankakee, IL 60901
(815) 939-0053
  Orville R. & Dorothy Reed
  Kankakee, Iroquois rivers

INDIANA

Clements Canoe Rentals &
Sales
911 Wayne Ave.
Crawfordsville, IN 47933
(317) 362-6272/9864
  Greg L. Woods
  Sugar Creek

Fluid Fun Canoe
Sales & Rentals
Rte. 1, Box 1B
Bristol, IN 46507
(219) 848-4279
  Terry & Janet Streib
  St. Joe, Pigeon rivers

Germany Bridge Canoe Trips
R. R. 3, Box 239
Rochester, IN 46975
(219) 223-2212
  Paul & Maxine Bardsley
  Tippecanoe River

Morgan's Brookville Canoe
Center
Box 118, Blue Creek Rd.
Brookville, IN 47012
(317) 647-4904
  Dirk & Starla Morgan
  Whitewater River

Root's Camp & Ski Haus
6844 N. Clinton (Hwy. 427)
Ft. Wayne, IN 46806
(219) 484-2604
    Jack H. Root

Stone Valley Canoe Livery &
Square Dance Barn
RR 3, Box 1
West Harrison, IN 47060
(812) 637-5183
    Tom & Carol Stone
    Whitewater River

Outdoor Adventures, Inc.
410 North Sixth St.
West Monroe, LA 71291
(318) 387-0128
    Nancy Caire
    LA, AR, MS

Pack and Paddle Tours &
Rental, Inc.
602 Pinhook Rd., East
Lafayette, LA 70501
(318) 232-5854
    Doug and Doris Waddell
    Whiskey, Chitto rivers

Springriver Corp.
5606 Randolph Rd.
Rockville, MD 20852
(301) 881-5696
    Bradley Reardon
    MD, VA, WV rivers

W.W. Outfitters, Inc.
P.O. Box 34564
W. Bethesda, MD 20817
(301) 251-9110
    W.G. Eicke
    Potomac and area rivers

KENTUCKY

The Knobs
535 Jackson St.
Campbellsville, KY 42718
(502) 465-3916/789-2266
    Robert P. Hightower
    Green River

Rockcastle Adventures
P.O. Box 662
London, KY 40741
(606) 864-9407 and 679-5026
    Rick & Sherri Egedi &
    Family
    *Rockcastle, Cumberland
    rivers*

Thaxton's South Fork Canoe
Trails
Rte. 2, Hays Station Rd.,
Box 391
Falmouth, KY 41040
(606) 654-5111
    Jim & Ann Thaxton
    *South Licking, Main
    Licking rivers*

LOUISIANA

Canoe & Trail Shop, Inc.
624 Moss Street
New Orleans, LA 70119
(504) 488-8528
    Byron Almquist

Oceans I, Mountains II
1300 West 21st Ave.
Covington, LA 70433
(504) 892-9647
    Hamilton L. Martin
    LA, MS, AL

MAINE

Allagash Wilderness Outfitters
Box 620, Star Rte. 76
Greenville, ME 04441
(207) 695-2821
    Rick Givens
    *Allagash, Penobscot,
    St. John rivers*

Saco River Canoe & Kayak,
Inc.
P.O. Box 111
Freyburg, ME 04037
(207) 935-2369
    Fred Westerberg
    Saco River

Sunrise City Canoe
Expeditions, Inc.
Cathance Lake, Rte. 191
Grove Post, ME 04638
(207) 454-7708
    Martin Brown
    *All rivers eastern and
    northern Maine*

MARYLAND

Hudson Bay Outfitters, Ltd.
16698 Oakmont Ave.
Gaithersburg, MD 20760
(301) 840-0650
    Hank Cohan

River & Trail Outfitters, Inc.
Box 246, Valley Rd.
Knoxville, MD 21758
(301) 834-9950
    Lee Baihly
    *Shenandoah, Potomac rivers
    and tributaries*

MASSACHUSETTS

Charles River Canoe Service
2401 Commonwealth Ave.
Newton, MA 02166
(617) 527-9885
    Larry Smith
    Charles River

New England Winemaking
Supply
501 Worchester Rd.
Framingham, MA 01701
(617) 875-1414
    Don O'Connor
    Eastern MA

Riverrun North, Inc.
Rte. 7, P.O. Box 636
Sheffield, MA 01257
(413) 528-1100
    John Pogue
    Housatonic River

MICHIGAN

Baldwin Canoe Rental
P.O. Box 265
Baldwin, MI 49304
(616) 745-4669
    Roger & Marcia Beilfuss
    Pere, Marquette, Pine rivers

Carl's Canoe Livery
10499 S. 15 Mi. Rd.,
Hoxeyville
Cadillac, MI 49601
(616) 797-5156 and 862-3402
    Carl & Betty Fortelka
    Pine River

Duggan's Canoe, Inc.
604 West Main St.
Harrison, MI 48625
(517) 539-7149
   Bill Duggan
   Big Muskegon River

Greenwood Campground
636 W. Greenwood Rd.
Alger, MI 48610
(517) 345-2778
   Ervin Schilke
   Rifle River

Happy Mohawk Canoe Livery
735 Fruitvale Rd.
Montague, MI 49437
(616) 894-4209
   Jim & Joy Cordray
   White River

Heavner Canoe Rental, Inc.
2775 Garden Rd.
Milford, MI 48042
(313) 685-2379
   Alan Heavner
   Huron River

Hiawatha Canoe Livery
1113 Lake St.
Roscommon, MI 48653
(517) 275-5213
   South Branch Ausable River

Hinchman Acres Resort &
Canoe Rental
Box 146
Mio, MI 48647
(517) 826-3991
   Sam & Natile Giardina
   Ausable River

Ivan's Canoe Rental
Box 787, M-37 So.
Baldwin, MI 49304
(616) 745-3361
   Bill Davis, Jr.
   Pere Marquette River

Marrik's Pine River Canoe
Service
7603 W. 50 Mile Rd.
Cadillac, MI 49601
(616) 862-3471
   Mark Miltner
   Pine River

Mountainside Canoe Livery
4700 W. Remus Rd.
Mt. Pleasant, MI 48858
(517) 772-5437
   John & Donna Buckley
   Chippewa River

North Cut Store and Canoe
Livery
Rte. 2, Box 366
Roscommon, MI 48653
(517) 821-9521
   Greg & Lynn Lefevere
   *Cut River, Higgins,
   Houghton lakes*

Northland Outfitters
Box 65
Germfask, MI 49836
(906) 586-9801
   Tom & Carma Gronback
   Manistigue, Foxgins rivers

Port O'Call Canoe Rental
4273 S. Straits Hwy.
Indian River, MI 49749
(616) 238-8181
   Scott B. Anderson
   *Stergeon, Pidgon, Indian
   rivers*

Riverbend Campground Canoe
Rental
864 North Main
Omer, MI 48749
(517) 653-2576
   Tom & Norma Somero
   Rifle River

Riverside Canoes, Inc.
Rte. 1
Honor, MI 49640
(616) 325-5622
   Tom Stocklen
   Platte River

Russell Canoes &
Campgrounds
146 Carrington
Omer, MI 48749
(517) 653-2644
   Robert & Leslie Russell
   Rifle River

Sawmill Canoe Livery
230 Baldwin St.
Big Rapids, MI 49307
(616) 796-0909
   Don Trites, Don DeWitt
   Big Muskegon River

Sawyer Canoe Co.
234 State St., P.O. Box 435
Oscoda, MI 48750
(517) 739-9181
   Bob Gramprie
   Ausable River

Skip's Huron River Canoe
Livery
3780 W. Delhi Rd.
Ann Arbor, MI 48103
(313) 769-8686
   Harold & Janet McDonald
   Huron River

Sport'N'Life Canoe Livery
18910 205th Avenue
Big Rapids, MI 49307
(616) 796-9284
   Don Nemec
   Big Muskegon River

Sportsman's Port Canoe
Camp
R.R. 1, W. Caberfae Hwy.
Wellston, MI 49689
(616) 862-3571
   Mary Barber
   *Pine, Big and Little
   Manistee rivers*

Sylvania Outfitters
West U.S. Hwy. 2
Watersmeet, MI 49969
(906) 358-4766
   Robert Zelinski
   *Sylvania tract, Ontonagon
   river system*

U-Rent-Em-Canoe Livery
221 E. Green St. (M-37)
Hastings, MI 49058
(616) 945-3191
   Michael J. Hawthorne
   Thornapple River

Vic's Canoes & Camping
Salmon Run, R.R. 2
Grant, MI 49327
(616) 834-5494
   Ray & Mary Ellen Spyker
   Muskegon River

MINNESOTA

Cliff Wold's Canoe Trip
Outfitting
1731 E. Sheridan
Ely, MN 55731
(218) 365-3267
Cliff Wold
*B.W.C.A., Quetico-
Superior*

Crane Lake Base Camp
Crane Lake, MN 55725
(218) 993-2396
Jeff & Joni Wartchow
*B.W.C.A., Quetico,
Superior Nat'l Forest,
Voyageur Nat'l Park*

Gunflint Northwoods
Outfitters, Inc.
Box 100 G.T.
Grand Marais, MN 55604
(218) 388-2294
Bruce Kerfoot
*B.W.C.A., Quetico-
Superior*

Jocko's Clearwater Canoe
Outfitters
Gunflint Trail, Box 31
Grand Marais, MN 55604
(218) 388-2254
Lee Nelson
*B.W.C.A., Quetico-
Superior*

Midwest Canoe Rental
3517 Skycroft Dr.
Minneapolis, MN 55418
(612) 484-9922
Don Heinrich
All Minnesota waters

Penquin Rents
4342 Colorado Ave., N.
Minneapolis, MN 55422
(612) 533-8768
Jim Hermansen
All MN rivers, B.W.C.A.

Rom's Canoe Country
Outfitters, Inc.
629 E. Sheridan St.,
P.O. Box 30
Ely, MN 55731
(218) 365-4046
Bob Olson
*B.W.C.A. in MN and
Quetico Pk., Canada*

Taylor Falls Canoe Rental
Box 225
Taylor Falls, MN 55084
(612) 465-6314 and 291-7980
Dennis Raedeke
St Croix, Namekagon rivers

Tip-of-the-Trail Canoe
Outfitters
Box 147, Gunflint Trail
Grand Marais, MN 55604
(218) 388-2225
Bill Douglas
*B.W.C.A., Quetico-
Superior*

Tom and Woods Moose Lake
Canoe Trips
Box 358
Ely, MN 55731
(218) 365-5837
*B.W.C.A., Quetico-
Superior*

MISSOURI

Akers Ferry Canoe Rental
Cedar Grove Rte., Box 90
Salem, MO 65560
(314) 858-3224
Eugene & Eleanor Maggard
Current River

Bass Canoe Rental
Box BB
Steelville, MO 65565
(314) 775-2954
Bob Bass
*Meramec Courtois, Huzzah
rivers*

Carr's Canoe Rental
Round Springs Rte.
Eminence, MO 65466
(314) 858-3240
Gary & Carol Smith
Current, Jacks, Fork rivers

Current River Canoe Rental
Gladden Star Rte.
Salem, MO 65560
(314) 858-3250
Allen Ramsey
Current River

H-V Canoe Rentals & Huzzah
Valley Stables and
Campground
S.R. 287, Box 64
Steelville, MO 65565
(314) 786-8412
William R. Cottrell
Huzzah, Courtois

Jack's Fork Canoe Rental
Rte. 1, Box 180
Eminence, MO 65466
(314) 226-3434
John Stewart &
Gene Maggard
Jacks, Fork, Current rivers

Jadwin Canoe Rental, Inc.
Jadwin, MO 65501
(314) 729-5229
Darrel & Shelia Blackwell
Current River

Markham Springs Canoe
Rental
Rte. 1
Mill Spring, MO 63952
(314) 998-2257
Kim Duckett
Black River

Meramec Canoe Rental
Rte. 4, Box 5
Sullivan, MO 63080
(314) 468-6519 and 468-6266
Doyle & Vicki Isom
Meramec River

Neil Canoe & Boat Rental
P.O. Box 396
Van Buren, MO 63965
(314) 323-4447
Roy Gossett
Current, Jacks, Fork rivers

Ray's Canoe Rental
Rte. 1, Box 277
Steelville, MO 65565
(314) 775-5697
Mike & Rose Hofstetter
Meramec River

Ray's Riverside Resort
Rte. 7, Box 417
Licking, MO 65542
(314) 674-2430 or 674-3931
Ray Wallace
Big Piney River

Silver Arrow Canoe Rental,
Inc.
Gladden Star Rte., Box 31
Salem, MO 65560
(314) 729-5770
George Purcell
Current, Jacks, Fork rivers

Sullivan's Round Springs
Canoe Rental
Gladden Star Rte.
Salem, MO 65560
(314) 858-3237
Billy Bland, Mgr.
Current River

Twin Bridges Canoe Rental
S.S. Rte., Box 230
West Plains, MO 65775
(417) 256-7507
Jan & Wendell Olmsted
*North Fork River, Bryant
Creek*

Two Rivers Canoe Rental,
Inc.
Rte. 2, Box 199
Eminence, MO 65466
(314) 226-3478
Joel Devall
Current, Jacks, Fork rivers

Wild River Canoe Rental
Gladden Star Rte., Box 60
Salem, MO 65560
(314) 858-3230
Jack & De Ann Patton
Current River

Windy's Canoe Rental
Box 151
Eminence, MO 65466
(314) 226-3404
Windy Smith
Current, Jacks, Fort rivers

MISSISSIPPI

Natchez Campground &
Canoe Park
Mississippi Hwy. 407 at
Big Black River
10 miles east of Winona
Winona, MS 38967
(504) 384-1725
Albert G. Sens
Big Black River

Okatoma Outdoor Post
Rte 2, Box 226-C
Sanford, MS 39479
(601) 722-4297/583-3174
Richard & Pattie Brantley
Okatoma River

Outward Bound Shop, Inc.
329 North 26th Ave.
Hattiesburg, MS 39401
(601) 582-1741
Bo Eakens
*Black Creek, Okatoma
Creek*

MONTANA

Pack-n-Paddle Canoe Rentals
Montana Rivers Canoe Livery
2940 Lewis Ave.
Billings, MT 59102
(406) 652-4384
Bob Hughes
Yellowstone Park and River

Yellowstone Canoe Livery
815 N. 2nd
Miles City, MT 59301
(406) 232-5250
Russell F. Penkal
Yellowstone River

NEBRASKA

Dryland Aquatics, Inc.
1832 North Park
Fremont, NE 68025
(402) 721-5801
Louis E. Christiansen
All rivers in Nebraska

Wilson Outfitters Nebraska
1329 Dawes Ave.
Lincoln, NE 68521
(402) 476-2300 (Nov. 1–Apr. 1)
(402) 497-3479 (Apr. 1–Nov. 1)
Loren Wilson
All Nebraska waters

NEW HAMPSHIRE

Saco Bound Northern Waters
Rte. 302, Box 113
Center Conway, NH 03813
(603) 447-2177
Ned McSherry
Saco, Androscoggin rivers

Wilderness Outfitters, Inc.
Rte. 101A
Milford, NH 03055
(603) 673-4211
Jim Wiedman
Souhegan, Nashua rivers

NEW JERSEY

Adams Canoe Rentals, Inc.
Atsion Lake – R.D. 2
Vincentown, NJ 08088
(609) 268-0189
R. Wayne Adams
Batsto, Mullica rivers

Art's Canoe Rental Cedar
Creek Campground, Inc.
1052 Rte. 9
Bayville, NJ 08721
(201) 269-1413
Debra Dingee &
Bill Fleming
Cedar Creek

Bel Haven Lake, Inc.
R.F.D. 2, Box 152A
Egg Harbor, NJ 08215
(609) 965-2031
Bill Bell
*Batsto, Mullica, Oswego,
Wading rivers*

Boats & Paddles
P.O. Box 441
Madison, NJ 07940
(201) 635-6593
Bill & Ann Sweeney
NJ, NY, CT, & PA rivers

Cranford Boat & Canoe Co.
250 Springfield Ave.
Cranford, NJ 07016
(201) 272-6991
Frank Betz

Indian Head Canoes
Box 106, R.D. 1
Lafayette, NJ 07848
(201) 383-3289
Tony Brunovsky
Delaware River

JJ's Landing, Inc.
22 Lakeside Rd., RD 2
Hewitt, NJ 07421
(201) 728-2177
Nancy Kolasa
Greenwood Lake

Lenape Park Recreation
Center
Park Rd., Box 57
Mays Landing, NJ 08330
(609) 625-2021
  Ed Young
  Egg Harbor River

Pineland Canoes, Inc.
RD 2, Box 212, Rte. 527
Jackson, NJ 08527
(201) 364-0389
  Ed Mason
  Toms River

Winding River Campground
RD 2, Box 246
Mays Landing, NJ 08330
(609) 625-3191
  Jim Horsey
  *Great Egg Harbor River,
  Lenape Lake*

NEW YORK

Algonquin Outfitters
402 Bonnie Brae Ave.
Rochester, NY 14618
(705) 635-2243
  Bill Swift
  *Oxtongue Lake, Dwight,
  Ontario, Canada P0A 1H0*

Barryville Kayak Inc.
Rte. 97
Barryville, NY 12719
(914) 557-6158
  Delaware River

Bob Landers Canoe Rental
R.D. 2
Narrowsburg, NY 12764
(914) 252-3925
  Bob & Rick Lander
  Delaware River

Canoe/Kayak Rentals of Long
Island
798 Old Dock Rd.
Kings Park, L.I., NY 11754
(516) 724-5433 and 269-9761
  Arnold DiScorsi &
  Bob Koliner
  *Nissequogue, Carmans,
  Peconic rivers*

Curt's Sporting Goods
Rte. 97
Sparrowbush, NY 12780
(914) 856-5024
  Delaware River

J & J Canoes, Inc.
Box 136
Narrowsburg, NY 12764
(914) 252-6824
  John & Josephine Kelly
  Delaware River

Pack & Paddle
600 W. 111th St. No. 12A
New York, NY 10025
(212) 864-2776
  Bruce Kaufstein
  NY, PA, NJ waters

Rivett's Boat Livery
Lake Trail
Old Forge, NY 13420
(315) 369-3123
  Richard & Barb Rivett
  Adirondack waters

Silver Canoe Rentals
37 S. Maple Ave.
Port Jervis, NY 12771
(914) 856-7055
  Jack March
  Delaware River

Three River Canoe Corp.
P.O. Box 7, Rte. 97
Pond Eddy, NY 12770
(914) 557-6078
  Jerry & Elizabeth Lovelace
  Delaware River

Tickner's Moose River Rentals
Riverside Drive
Old Forge, NY 13420
(315) 369-6286
  Dan & Natalie Tickner
  Moose River

Top Hat Car Wash Co., Inc.
89 Peconic Ave.
Riverhead, NY 11901
(516) 727-9895
  James A. Dreeben
  Peconic River and Bay

Upper Delaware Campground,
Inc.
Box 331
Callicoon, NY 12723
(914) 887-5344 and
(516) 599-3578
  Al Kaufmann
  Delaware River

White Water Canoe
River Rd., Rte. 97
Barryville, NY 12719
(914) 557-8178
  Brian Acciavatti
  Delaware River

Wild & Scenic River Tours &
Rentals
Rte. 97
Barryville, NY 12719
(914) 557-8783
  Jules Robinson
  Delaware River

NORTH CAROLINA

Nantahala Outdoor Center,
Inc.
U.S. 19 W., Box 41
Bryson City, NC 28713
(704) 488-2175
  *Nantahala, Chattooga,
  Ocoee, French Broad,
  Nolichucky*

Nantahala Rafts, Inc.
Star Rte, Box 70 N.
Bryson City, NC 28713
(704) 488-3854 (Nov.–Apr.)
(704) 488-2325 (May–Oct.)
  Keith Maddox
  Nantahala River

New River Outfitters, Inc.
P.O. Box 433
Jefferson, NC 28640
(919) 246-7711
  James Wuenscher
  *New, Toe, Nolichucky
  rivers*

River Runners Emporium
1209 W. Main St.
Durham, NC 27701
(919) 688-2001
  H.M. Dubose, Jr.
  *Central North Carolina
  waters*

Rolling Thunder River Co.,
Inc.
Box 88
Almond, NC 28702
(704) 488-2030
   Gary Duven
   Chattooga, Ocoee,
   Nolichucky, Nantahala,
   Rio Grande

Zaloo's Canoes
Rte. 1
Jefferson, NC 28640
(919) 246-3066
   Jedd Farrington
   New River

OHIO

Blackhand Gorge Canoe &
Ski Shop
11101 Staddens Bridge Rd.
Newark, OH 43055
(614) 763-4000
Manual Beltran
   Ernest & Liz Grimm
   Licking River

Camp Hi Canoe Livery
12275 Abbott Rd.
Hiram, OH 44234
(216) 569-7621
   George Hazlett
   Cuyahoga River

Carlisle Canoe Center
State Rte. 416 So., Box 161
New Philadelphia, OH 44663
(216) 339-4010 and
(216) 339-3805 (Res.)
   Glenn & Leah Carlisle
   Tuscarawas River, Sugar
   Creek

Ft. Amanda Canoe Livery
Rte. 4
Cridersville, OH 45806
(419) 657-6782
   Darrell & Maxine Barnes
   Auglaize River

Fyffe's Canoe Rental
3234 Washington Rd.
Bellbrook, OH 45305
(513) 848-4812
   Charles B. Fyffe
   Little Miami, Mad rivers

Hocking Valley Canoe Livery
31251 Chieftan Dr.
Logan, OH 43138
(614) 385-8685 and 385-2503
   Lewis Barbini
   Hocking River
   Two Locations: Logan and
   Nelsonville

Loudonville Canoe Livery
424 West Main St.
Loudonville, OH 44842
(419) 994-4561
   Michael Schafrath
   Blackfork, Mohican, Clear
   Fork rivers

Mohican Canoe Livery
P.O. Box 263, State Rte. 3
Loudonville, OH 44842
(419) 994-4097
   Doug Shannon
   Blackfork, Mohican,
   Walhounding rivers

Mohican River Canoe Livery
P.O. Box 292, St. Rte. 3 S.
Loudonville, OH 44842
(419) 994-4020
   Patty Shannon
   Blackfork, Mohican rivers

Morgan's Fort Ancient Canoe
Livery
2247 Moor-Saur Rd., St. Rte. 350
Morrow, OH 45152
(513) 932-7658 and 899-2166
   Bob, June, Gary Morgan
   Little Miami River

Morgan's Mad River Outpost
5605 Lower Valley Pike
Springfield, OH 45502
(513) 882-6925
   Jay Joyce
   Mad River

NTR Canoe Livery, Inc.
State Rte. 212, P.O. Box 203
Bolivar, OH 44612
(216) 874-2002 and 484-4295
   Tim & Ann Swain
   Tuscarawas River

Pleasant Hill Canoe Livery,
Inc.
P.O. Box 10
Perrysville, OH 44864
(419) 938-7777
   Bob, Mel & Ken Reinthal
   Blackfork, Mohican,
   Walhounding rivers

Raccoon Creek Canoe Livery
Box 330
Rio Grande, OH 45674
(614) 245-5304
   Raccoon Creek

Rainbow Adventures Canoe
Rental
1610 Upper Valley Pike
Springfield, OH 45504
(513) 322-1432 and
(614) 852-4813 (off season)
   Lester Barnhart
   Mad, Little Miami rivers

River. Run Canoe Livery
191 E. Ford Ave.
Barberton, OH 44203
(216) 745-8109
   Lois Lucille Hout
   Tuscarawas River

Three Rivers Canoe Livery
SR 36 & 83 Lake Park Rd.
Coshocton, OH 43812
(614) 622-4080
   Mike Halco
   Mohican, Walhounding,
   Muskingum rivers

Trapper John's Canoe Livery
7141 London-Groveport Rd.
Grove City, OH 43123
(614) 877-4321
   Big Darby Creek

Treasure Island Canoe Livery
439 North Elm St.
Troy, OH 45373
(513) 339-5555
   Great Miami River

OKLAHOMA

Sparrow Hawk Camps
Loop Rte.
Tahlequah, OK 74464
(918) 456-8371
   Carl George
   Illinois River

OREGON

Brown's Landing
Rte. 3, Box 134
Scappoose, OR 97056
(503) 543-6526
Jerry & Joan Blair
Multnomah Channel

Frontier River Trips
9039 Lower River Rd.
Grants Pass, OR 97526
(503) 474-0979
Glenn A. Lewman, Jr.
Illinois, Rogue, Klamath

Galice Raft Trips
P.O. Box 638
Merlin, OR 97532
(503) 476-8051
Paul Brooks
Rogue River

Juniper Guide Service &
Outfitters
Rte. 1, Box 273
Powell Butte, OR 97753
(503) 447-6528
Dave McCourtney
*Deschutes, Day, Oregon
rivers*

Leierer's Wilderness Outfitting
934 Hylo Rd., SE
Salem, OR 97306
(503) 581-2803
Chuck, Nita & Cheri Leierer
Willamette River

Lifetime Paddle Sport
P.O. Box 7181
Eugene, OR 97401
(503) 747-4948
Kurt Renner

Sportcraft Marina
1701 Clackamette Dr.
Oregon City, OR 97045
(503) 656-6484
Larry J. Bigbee
*Willamette, Clackamas
rivers*

PENNSYLVANIA

Adventure Tours, Inc.
P.O. Box 631
Stroudsburg, PA 18360
(717) 223-0505
John & Wendy Jacobi
Delaware River

Allegheny Outfitters
RD 1, Box 1730
Russell, PA 16345
(814) 757-8801
Michael R. Dipenti, Jr.
*Allegheny River and
Reservoir, Tionesta Creek*

Canoe, Kayak & Sailing Craft
712 Rebecca
Wilkinsburg, PA 15221
(412) 371-4802
Doug & Nancy Ettinger
Allegheny River

Chamberlain Canoes, Inc.
1527 Spruce St.
Stroudsburg, PA 18360
(717) 421-0180
Jim & Judy Chamberlain
Delaware River

Cook Forest Canoe Livery
Rte. 36, Cook Forest St. Pk.
Cooksburg, PA 16217
(814) 744-8094
Carl Lipford
Clarion River

Cushetunk Campground
Canoe Rental
Box 3
Milanville, PA 18443
(717) 729-7984
Jim Card
Delaware River

Deliverance Lifetime Sports
2 West Southern Ave.
S. Williamsport, PA 17701
(717) 322-8066
Ned Coates
*Pine, Pycoming, Loyalsock
creeks*

Doe Hollow Canoe Rentals,
Inc.
R.D. 2, Dept. NA
Bangor, PA 18013
(215) 498-5103
Paul & Jim Healey
Delaware, Penquest rivers

Evergreen Outdoor Center
P.O. Box 3081
Shiremanstown, PA 17011
(717) 737-4540
Bill Nesbit
GeoAnne E. Downing
*Delaware, Susquehanna
rivers and their tributaries*

Indian Valley Campground
Canoe Livery
P.O. Box 36
West Hickory, PA 16370
(814) 755-3578
Dick Farrer
Allegheny River

Kittatinny Canoes, Inc.
At Dingman's Bridge
Dingmans Ferry, PA 18328
(717) 828-2700
Frank & Ruth Jones
Delaware River

Love's Canoe Rental
Star Rte., Box 17, Boot Jack
Rd.
Ridgeway, PA 15853
(814) 776-6285
Dave Love
*Clarion, Susquehanna,
Allegheny rivers*

Mountain Streams Trails
Outfitters
Box 106
Ohiopyle, PA 15470
(412) 329-8810 or
(800) 245-4090
*Youghiogheny, Cheat,
Gauley rivers*

Northbrook Canoe Company
1810 Beagle Rd.
West Chester, PA 19380
(215) 793-2279
Zeke Hubbard
Brandywine River

Northland Canoe Outfitters
R.D. 7, Box 7765
Stroudsburg, PA 18360
(717) 223-0275
Harry Snow
Delaware River

Pack Shack Adventures, Inc.
Broad St., P.O. Box 127
Delaware Wtr. Gp., PA 18327
(717) 424-8533
John C. Greene
Delaware River

Penrods' Canoe & River
Adventures
RD 1, Box 93
Summerhill, PA 15958
(814) 487-4164
Bruce Penrod
*Waters of S.W. PA, Stoney
Creek, Youghiogheny River*

Point Pleasant Canoe Rental
& Sales
P.O. Box 6
Pt. Pleasant, PA 18950
(215) 297-8400
Thomas W. McBrien
Delaware River, Tohickon Creek

River Paths Outfitters
RD 1, Box 15-B
Confluence, PA 15424
(814) 395-3136 and
(412) 225-2030
Jim Prothero & Jim Wilson
Youghiogheny, Casselman rivers

Stefan's Lagoon Livery
297 W. Market
Clearfield, PA 16830
(814) 765-6725 and 838-1771
Lou Stefan
Presque Isle Bay, Susquehanna River

Susquehanna Canoe Rentals,
Inc.
RD 4, Box 319
Mountaintop, PA 18707
(717) 283-0318
Gerald Shumbris
Susquehanna River

Tri-Rivers Canoes
626 Elm St., P.O. Box 279
Tionesta, PA 16353
(814) 755-4577
Hugh & Pat Keating
Allegheny River

Tri-State Canoe Rentals
Rte. 209, Box 310
Dingmans Ferry, PA 18328
(717) 828-2510
Chuck & Judy Shay
Delaware River

Tussey Mt. Outfitters
P.O. Box 465
Boalsburg, PA 16827
(814) 466-7457
Also: 600 St. Rd., Rte. 15
Marysville, PA 17053
All of central PA, Juniata, Susquehanna, Pine and Penns creeks

Water Gap Canoe Inc.
Rte. 611, Box 213
Delaware Wtr. Gp., PA 18327
(717) 476-0398
Brian Martin
Delaware River

Wiggers Canoe & Kayak Sales
RD 4, Box 452
Corry, PA 16407
(814) 664-2783 and 454-0520
Dave & Pat Wiggers
French Creek, Allegheny River

SOUTH CAROLINA

Chattooga Whitewater Shop
Hwy. 76
Long Creek, SC 29658
(803) 647-9083
Bruce Hare
Chattooga River

TENNESSEE

Buffalo River Canoe Rental,
Inc.
Flatwoods, TN 38458
(615) 589-2755
Alf Ashton, Jr.
Buffalo River

The Canoe & Camp Shop
P.O. Box 306
Norris, TN 37828
(615) 494-0725
Joann Doub
Clinch River, Horris Lake

Ocoee Outdoors
P.O. Box 172
Ocoee, TN 37361
(615) 338-2438
Bob Baker & J.T. Lemons
Ocoee, Hiawassee rivers

Sunburst Wilderness
Adventures, Inc.
P.O. Box 329 N
Benton, TN 37307
(615) 338-3388
Marc Hunt

Wild River Adventures, Inc.
226 N. Main St.
Clinton, TN 37716
(615) 457-3232
Charles Winfrey
Obed, Big South Fork, Cumberland rivers

TEXAS

Abbott's River Outfitters
Star Rte. 3, Box 871
New Braunfels, TX 78130
(512) 625-4928
Steve & Jane Abbott
Guadalupe River

Casey Ridge Canoes
Rte. 1, Box 421 E
New Caney, TX 77357
(713) 540-1135
R.P. "Bob" Daigle
East Texas & Lake Houston Wilderness outfitting

High Trails Canoe Co.
12421 N. Central Expwy.
Dallas, TX 75243
(214) 661-3943
Bob Narramore
All TX, OK, and AR rivers

Texas Canoe Trails, Inc.
121 River Terrace
New Braunfels, TX 78130
(512) 964-3760
Wayne Walls
Rio Grande, Guadalupe rivers

Turkey Springs Resort
Star Rte. 3, Box 176-G
Canyon Lake, TX 78130
(512) 964-3636
Johnnie Bezdek, Jr.
Guadalupe River

Whitewater Sports
Star Rte. 3, Box 22
Canyon Lake, TX 78130
(512) 964-3800
Ellen Martin
Guadalupe River

The Workshop
Rte. 3, Box 1
Bandera, TX 78003
(512) 796-3553
Fred Collins
Medina River

UTAH

Rent-A-Raft
3690 East, 7000 So., Suite 101
Salt Lake City, UT 84121
(801) 942-6669
Colorado River

Tag-A-Long Tours, Inc.
P.O. Box 1206
Moab, UT 84532
(800) 453-3292
Mitch Williams
Colorado, Green rivers

VIRGINIA

Clore Bros. Outfitters
Rte. 1, Box 34-C
Fredericksburg, VA 22401
(703) 786-7749 and 594-2918
Gene & Linda Clore
Rappahannock, Rapidan rivers

Front Royal Canoe Co.
P.O. Box 473
Front Royal, VA 22630
(703) 635-2741 and 636-1744
Don Roberts
Shenandoah River

Kelly's Ford Outfitters
P.O. Box 273, Bus. Rte. 29 So.
Remington, VA 22734
(703) 439-8740
Ronald W. Meadows
Rappahannock-Rapidan Watershed

Little River Leisure Enterprises
P.O. Box 83
Doswell, VA 23047
(804) 227-3401
Chuck Martin
Little, Ann, Pamunkey rivers

Rappahannock Canoes, Inc.
1209 Powhatan St.
Fredericksburg, VA 22401
(703) 371-5085
Bill Micks
Rappahannock, Anna, Rapidan, Mataponi

Shenandoah River Outfitters, Inc.
R.F.D. 3
Luray, VA 22835
(703) 743-4159
Shenandoah River

Wild River Outfitters, Inc.
5921 Churchland Blvd.
Portsmouth, VA 23703
(804) 484-7330
Kim P. Whitley
Appomattox, Nottoway rivers

VERMONT

Canoe Imports, Inc.
RD 3, Box 2000, Rte. 7
Shelburne, VT 05482
(802) 985-2992
Bob & Barb Schumacher
VT rivers and lakes

WASHINGTON

Base Camp, Inc.
901 W. Holly St.
Bellingham, WA 98225
(906) 733-5461
Frank Schultz

Family Sports
813 E. Tacoma
Ellensburg, WA 98926
(509) 925-9117
Bert Shook
Yakima River

Pacific Water Sports
16205 Pacific Hwy. So.
Seattle, WA 98188
(206) 246-9385
Lee & Judy Moyer
Pacific N.W. and Canada waters

WISCONSIN

Brule River Canoe Rental
Box 145N
Brule, WI 54820
(715) 372-4983
Brian & Pamela Carlson
Brule River

Herb's Wolf River Raft Rental
Hwy. 55 Wild Wolf Inn
White Lake, WI 54491
(715) 882-8612
Herbert Buettner
Wolf River

Kickapoo River Canoe Rental
Rte. 2, Box 210A
Lafarge, WI 54639
(608) 625-2252
Jack Lee
Kickapoo River

River Forest Rafts
White Lake, WI 54491
(715) 882-3351 or
(414) 499-7587
Jim & Maryann Stecher
Wolf River

Riverview Hills Canoe Rentals
Rte. 1, Box 307
Muscoda, WI 53573
(608) 739-3472
Albert J. Bremmer
Wisconsin, Pine rivers

Steed's Wolf River Lodge, Inc.
White Lake, WI 54491
(715) 882-2182
George Steed
Wolf, Peshtigo rivers

Whitewater Specialties
P.O. Box 157 (Hwy. 55)
White Lake, WI 54491
(715) 882-5400
Bill Kallner
Wolf, Peshtigo rivers

Planning a Canoe Trip

Planning can be as much fun as the actual trip itself. It can take months of detailed exploration into the area in which you are interested. This includes information concerning natural wonders, rivers, ponds, lakes, streams, rivers, and oceans. Research will include letters to the local chambers of commerce and the state department of conservation, reading of regional publications, and thumbing through national magazines for articles on the particular waters of each location. Then you should write to all the outfitters and resorts in the area you have selected to get their views on the possibilities, costs, and dates, and also what general equipment will be needed.

Included here is a list of information sources you should look into. Start a file now. In years to come it will be invaluable.

SOURCES OF OUTDOOR INFORMATION

The following list has been compiled for a ready source of up-to-date information on states, their laws and in many cases free booklets on where to go for each species of game fish. This information may be had for the asking.

Alabama—Department of Conservation, Administrative Building, Montgomery, AL 36101.

Alaska—Department of Fish and Game, 229 Alaska Office Building, Juneau, AK 99801.

Arizona — State Game and Fish Commission, Arizona State Building, Phoenix, AZ 85000.

Arkansas — State Game and Fish Commission, Game and Fish Building, State Capitol Grounds, Little Rock, AK 72200.

California — Department of Fish and Game, 722 Capitol Avenue, Sacramento, CA 95801.

Colorado — State Game and Fish Department, 1530 Sherman St., Denver, CO 80200.

Connecticut — State Board of Fisheries and Game, State Office Building, Hartford, CT 06100.

Delaware — Board of Game and Fish Commissioners, Dover, DE 19901.

District of Columbia — Metropolitan Police, Washington, DC 20000.

Florida — Game and Fresh Water Fish Commission, 646 W. Tennessee, Tallahassee, FL 32301.

Georgia — State Game and Fish Commission, 401 State Capitol, Atlanta, GA 30300.

Hawaii — Board of Commissioners of Agriculture and Forestry, Division of Fish and Game, Box 5425, Pawaa Substation, Honolulu, HI 96800.

Idaho — Department of Fish and Game, 518 Front St., Boise, ID 83700.

Illinois — Department of Conservation, State Office Building, Springfield, IL 62700.

Indiana — Department of Conservation, Division of Fish and Game, 311 W. Washington St., Indianapolis, IN 46200.

Iowa — State Conservation Commission, E. 7th & Court Ave., Des Moines, IA 50300.

Kansas — Forestry, Fish and Game Commission, Box 591, Pratt, KS 67124.

Kentucky — Department of Fish and Wildlife Resources, State Office Building, Annex, Frankfort, KY 40601.

Louisiana — Wild Life and Fisheries Commission, 126 Civil Courts Building, New Orleans, LA 70100.

Maine — Department of Inland Fisheries and Game, State House, Augusta, ME 04330.

Maryland — Maryland Game and Inland Fish Commission, State Office Building, Annapolis, MD 21400.

Massachusetts — Department of Natural Resources, Division of Fisheries and Game, 73 Tremont St., Boston, MA 02100.

Michigan — Department of Conservation, Lansing, MI 48900.

Minnesota — Department of Conservation, State Office Building, St. Paul, MN 55100.

Mississippi — State Game and Fish Commission, Woolfolk State Office Building, Jackson, MS 39200.

Missouri — State Conservation Commission, Farm Bureau Building, Jefferson City, MO 65101.

Montana — State Fish and Game Commission, Helena, MT 59601.

Nebraska — Game, Forestation and Parks Commission, State Capitol Building, Lincoln, NE 68500.

Nevada — State Fish and Game Commission, Box 678, Reno, NV 89500.

New Hampshire — State Fish and Game Department, 34 Bridge St., Concord, NH 03301.

New Jersey — Department of Conservation and Economic Development, Division of Fish and Game, 230 W. State St., Trenton, NJ 08600.

New Mexico — State Department of Game and Fish, Santa Fe, NM 87501.

New York — State Conservation Department, Albany, NY 12200.

North Carolina — Wildlife Resources Commission, Box 2919, Raleigh, NC 27600.

North Dakota — State Game and Fish Department, Bismarck, ND 58501.

Ohio — Department of Natural Resources, Wildlife Division, Ohio Department Building, Columbus, OH 43200.

Oklahoma — Department of Wildlife Conservation, Room 118, State Capitol Building, Oklahoma City, OK 73100.

Oregon — State Fish Commission, 307 State Office Building, Portland, OR 97200.

Pennsylvania — State Fish Commission, Harrisburg, PA 17101.

Rhode Island — Department of Agriculture and Conservation, Veterans Memorial Building, 83 Park St., Providence, RI 02900.

South Carolina — State Wildlife Resources Department, 1015 Main St., Box 360, Columbia, SC 29200.

South Dakota — State Department of Game, Fish and Parks, State Office Building, Pierre, SD 57501.

Tennessee — State Game and Fish Commission, Cordell Hull Building, Nashville, TN 37200.

Texas — State Game and Fish Commission, Austin, TX 78700.

Utah — State Department of Fish and Game, 1596 W. N. Temple, Salt Lake City, UT 84100.

Vermont — State Fish and Game Commission, Montpelier, VT 05602.

Virginia — Commission of Game and Inland Fisheries, 7 N. 2nd St., Box 1642, Richmond, VA 23200.

Washington — Department of Game, 600 N. Capitol Way, Olympia, WA 98501.

West Virginia — State Conservation Commission, State Office Building, No. 3, Charleston, WV 25300.

Wisconsin — State Conservation Department, State Office Building, Madison, WI 53700.

Wyoming — State Game and Fish Commission, Box 378, Cheyenne, WY 82001.

MAPS THAT AID THE ANGLER

The United States government offers us the finest maps available. Each state is divided into small areas, and a separate map is available for each. Each stream, river, and lake is shown in detail as are dirt roads and little-known access areas.

For maps east of the Mississippi River, contact the Geological Survey, Washington, D.C. West of the Mississippi, contact Geological Survey, Federal Center, Denver, Colorado.

Index maps of each state are available, free. These show all the quadrangles available for each area. From these master maps you may choose the individual area you wish to canoe — then order it, by number, from Geological Survey.

National Canoe Associations

American Canoe Association, 4260 East Evans Avenue, Denver, CO 80222. $6.00 per year for adult voting members plus $1.00 initiation fee: *Canoe* magazine, books and leaflets on canoeing, routes, general information, local clubs, races, and regattas.

American Whitewater Affiliation, P.O. Box 1584, San Bruno, CA 94066.

The Canadian Canoe Association, 805 Valetta Street, London N6H 2Z2 ON. $5.00 per year: general information, reports on canoe routes.

Fédération Québécoise de Canot-Kayak, Inc., 881 Boulevard de Maison-neuve Est. Montréal 132, PQ. Federation of local clubs. $25 per year: *Guide des Rivières du Québec* (Éditions du Jour, Montréal), specific canoe routes for members, non-profit workshop for improving canoe design and construction.

Izaak Walton League of America, 13711 Parkland Drive, Rockville, MD 20853.

National Audubon Society, 950 Third Avenue, New York, NY 10022. $15 per year, family membership: *Audubon* (semimonthly), workshops with local clubs.

Sierra Club, P.O. Box 7959, Rincon Annex, San Francisco, CA 94120. $22.50 per year, family membership, plus $5.00 admission fee: monthly magazine, bulletin, discounts on publications, guides to hiking and camping, illustrated books, organized wilderness trips, environmental issues.

The Wilderness Society, 729 Fifteenth Street, NW, Washington DC 20005. $7.50 per year: *The Living Wilderness* (quarterly), organized wilderness trips including canoeing, information on conservation.

Local Canoe Clubs

CANADA

North West Voyageurs
10922 88th Ave.
Edmonton 61, AB

UNITED STATES

California
Cakara
675 Overhill Dr.
Redding 96001

Feather River Kayak Club
1733 Broadway St.
Marysville 95901

Haystackers Whitewater
Canoe Club
P.O. Box 675
Kernville 93238

Marin Canoe Club
744 Penny Royal La.
San Rafael 94903

Powell Boating Club—
University of California
Berkeley
5499 Claremont Ave.
Oakland 94618

Sierra Club—
Loma Prieta Paddlers
85 Blake Ave.
Santa Clara 95051

Sierra Club Yokut R.T.S.
914 Standord Ave.
Modesto 95350

Southern California Canoe
Association
3966 South Menlo Ave.
Los Angeles 90037

Valley Canoe Club
10363 Calvin Ave.
Los Angeles 90025

YMCA Whitewater Club
640 North Center St.
Stockton 95202

Colorado
Colorado Whitewater
Association
2007 Mariposa
Boulder 80302

Fib Ark Boat Races, Inc.
P.O. Box 762
Salida 81201

Connecticut
Amston Lake Canoe Club
Deepwood Dr.
Amston 06231

Columbia Canoe Club
Lake Rd.
Columbia 06237

Waterford Canoe Club
Box 111
Waterford 06385

Delaware
Wilmington Trail Club
324 Spalding Rd.
Wilmington 19803

District of Columbia
Canoe Cruisers Association
6400 MacArthur Blvd.
Washington 20016

Potomac Boat Club
3530 Water St., NW
Washington 20007

Washington Canoe Club
3700 K St., NW
Washington 20007

Florida
Everglades Canoe Club
239 NE 20th St.
Delray Beach 33440

Florida Sport Paddling Club
133 Hickory La.
Seffner 33584

Seminole Canoe & Yacht Club
5653 Windermere Dr.
Jacksonville 32211

Georgia
Explorer Post 49
1506 Brawley Circle
Atlanta 30313

Georgia Canoeing Association
2816 De Foors Ferry Rd.
Atlanta 30318

Hawaii
Hawaii Kayak Club
1560 Murphy St.
Honolulu 96819

International Hawaiian Canoe
Association
1638A Kona
Honolulu 96814

Idaho
Idaho Alpine Club
1953 Melobu
Idaho Falls 83401

Sawtooth Wildwater Club
1255 Elm St.
Mountain Home 83647

Illinois
American Indian Center
Canoe Club
1630 North Wilson Ave.
Chicago 60640

Belleville Whitewater Club
3 Oakwood
Belleville 62223

Chicago Whitewater
Association
5652 South California Ave.
Chicago 60629

Illinois Paddling Council
2316 Prospect Ave.
Wanston 60201

Lincoln Park Boat Club
2236 North Burling St.
Chicago 60614

Prairie Club Canoeists
17 West 373 Belden
Addison 60101

Prairie State Canoeists
6320 North Hermitage Ave.
Chicago 60626

University of Chicago
Whitewater Club
933 East 56th St.
Chicago 60637

Indiana
Connersville Canoe Club
R.R. 3
Connersville 47331

Elkhart YMCA Canoe Club
229 West Franklin St.
Elkhart 46514

Hoosier Canoe Club
5641 North Delaware
Indianapolis 46220

Kekionga Voyageurs
1407 Kensington Blvd.
Fort Wayne 46805

St. Joe Valley Canoe &
Kayak Club
229 West Franklin
Elkhart 46514

Kansas
Johnson County Canoe Club
7832 Rosewood La.
Prairie Village 66208

Kentucky
Viking Canoe Club
3108 Rockaway Dr.
Louisville 40216

Maine
Penobscot Paddle & Chowder
Association
Box 121
Stillwater 04489

Maryland
Baltimore Kayak Club
7118 McLean Blvd.
Baltimore 01234

Monocacy Canoe Club
Route 1
Walkersville 21793

Massachusetts
A.M.C. Berkshire
33 Knollwood Dr.
East Longmeadow 01028

Cochituate Canoe Club
99 Dudley Rd.
Cochituate 01760

Foxboro Canoe Club
32 Taunton St.
Bellingham 02019

Lake Chaogg Canoe Club
P.O. Box 512
Webster 01570

Waupanoag Paddlers
345 Forest St.
Pembrook 02359

Westfield River Whitewater
Canoe Club
90 West Silver St.
Westfield 01085

Michigan
Kalamazoo Downstreamers
6820 Evergreen
Kalamazoo 49002

Lower Michigan Paddling
Council
8266 Patton
Detroit 48228

Michigan Canoe Race
Association
4735 Hillcrest
Trenton 48183

Michigan Trailfinders Club
2680 Rockhill, NE
Grand Rapids 49505

Niles Kayak Club
Route 1, Box 83
Buchanan 49107

Minnesota
Minnesota Canoe Association,
Inc.
Box 14177
Union Station
Minneapolis 55414

Missouri
AYH – Ozark Area
P.O. Box 13099
St. Louis 63119

Central Missouri State College
Outing Club
Department of Biology
Warrensburg 64093

Meramec River Canoe Club
3636 Oxford Blvd.
Maplewood 63143

Ozark Wilderness Waterways
Club
Box 8165
Kansas City 64112

Nebraska
Fort Kearney Canoeists
2623 Avenue D
Kearney 68847

Nevada
Basic High School Canoe
Club
751 Palo Verde Dr.
Henderson 89015

New Hampshire
Androscoggin Canoe & Kayak
Club
Lancaster 03584

Ledyard Canoe Club of
Dartmouth
Robinson Hall
Hanover 03755

Mad Pemi Canoe Club
93 Realty
Campton 03223

New Jersey
Knickerbocker Canoe Club
6115 Washington St.
West New York 07093

Mohawk Canoe Club
11 Thomas St.
High Bridge 08829

Murray Hill Canoe Club
Bell Telephone Labs
Murray Hill 07974

Neversink Canoe Sailing
Society
Oak Tree La.
Rumson 07760

Red Dragon Canoe Club
221 Edgewater Ave.
Edgewater Park 08010

New Mexico
Albuquerque Whitewater Club
804 Warm Sands Dr., SE
Albuquerque 87112

New York
Adirondack Mountain Club
Hamburg Savings Bank
315 Wykcoff Ave.
Brooklyn 11227

Adirondack Mountain Club
769 John Glenn Rd.
Webster 14580

A.M.C. – New York
Canoe Commission
Midland So. Box 1956
Syosset 11791

AYH – New York
6 Cardinal Ct.
West Nyack 10994

Inwood Canoe Club
509 West 212th St.
New York 10034

Ka Na Wa Ke Canoe Club
26 Pickwick Rd.
Dewitt (Syracuse) 13214

KCC – Cooperstown
Riverbrink
Cooperstown 13326

KCC – New York
6 Winslow Ave.
East Brunswick 08816

New York–New Jersey River
Conference Canoe & Kayak
Council
564 River Rd.
Chatham, NJ 07928

Niagara Gorge Kayak Club
147 Lancaster Ave.
Buffalo 14322

Sebago Canoe Club
9622 Avenue M
Brooklyn 11236

Sierra Club – Canoe
Commission
875 West 181st St.
New York 10033

Tasca
P.O. Box 41
Oakland Gardens 11364

Wanda Canoe Club
315 Cross St.
Fort Lee, NJ 07024

Wellsville Downriver Paddlers
Proctor Rd.
Wellsville 14895

Yonkers Canoe Club
360 Edwards Pl.
Yonkers 10701

North Carolina
Carolina Canoe Club
121 Turner St.
Elkin 20621

Ohio
AYH—Columbus
565 Old Farm Rd.
Columbus 43213

CMAC Kayak & Canoe Club
35124 Euclid Ave.
Willoughby 44094

Dayton Canoe Club
1020 Riverside Dr.
Dayton 45405

Keelhaulers Canoe Club
1649 Allen Dr.
Westlake 44145

Madhatters Canoe Club
2647 Norway
Perry 44081

Warner & Swasey Canoe Club
406 Mill Ave., SW
New Philadelphia 44663

Oklahoma
O K Canoers
3112 Chaucer Dr.
Village 73120

Tulsa Canoe & Camping Club
5810 East 30th Pl.
Tulsa 74114

Oregon
Mary Kayak Club
3312 Elmwood Dr., NW
Cornwallis 97330

Oregon Kayak & Canoe Club
2955 NE 49
Portland 97213

Pennsylvania
Allegheny Canoe Club
362½ Circle St.
Franklin 16323

A.M.C. Delaware Valley
306 Crestview Circle
Media 19063

AYH—Delaware Valley
4714 York Rd.
Philadelphia 19141

AYH—Pittsburgh
6300 Fifth Ave.
Pittsburgh 15232

Benscreek Canoe Club
R.D. 5, Box 256
Johnstown 15905

Bucknell Outing Club
Box C-1610
Bucknell University
Lewisburg 17837

Buck Ridge Ski Club
1728 Earlington Rd.
Havertown 19083

Delaware Canoe Club
14 South 14th St.
Easton 18042

Endless Mountain Voyageurs
285 Shorthill Rd.
Clarks Green 18411

Explorer Post 65
22 Catalpa Pl.
Pittsburgh 15228

Fox Chapel Canoe Club
610 Squaw Run Rd.
Pittsburgh 15238

Indiana University Outing
Club
Department of Chemistry
Indiana 15701

Kishacoquillas Canoe &
Rafting Club
c/o Wilderness Voyageurs
P.O. Box 97
Ohiopyle 15470

Mohawk Canoe Club
6 Canary Rd.
Levittown 19057

North Hills YMCA
Whitewater Club
1130 Sandlewood La.
Pittsburgh 15237

Oil Creek Valley Canoe Club
214 North First St.
Titusville 16354

Paoli Troop I, BSA
432 Strafford Ave.
Wayne 19087

Penn Hills Whitewater Canoe
Club
Penn Hills Senior High School
12200 Garland Dr.
Pittsburgh 15235

Penn State Outing Club
118 South Buckhout St.
University Park 16801

Philadelphia Canoe Club
4900 Ridge Ave.
Philadelphia 19128

Post 42, BSA
Route 2
Palmerton 19053

Scudder Falls Wildwater Club
795 River Rd.
Yardley 19067

Shenango Valley Canoe Club
863 Bechtal Ave.
Sharon 16146

Sylvan Canoe Club
132 Arch St.
Verona 15147

Wildwater Boating Club
Lock Box 179
Bellefonte 16823

Williamsport YMCA Canoe
Club
343 West 4th St.
Williamsport 17701

South Carolina
Sierra Club—Canoe Section
P.O. Box 463
Clemson 29631

Tennessee
Bluff City Canoe Club
P.O. Box 4523
Memphis 38104

Carbide Canoe Club
104 Ulena La.
Oak Ridge 37830

East Tennessee Whitewater
Club
P.O. Box 3074
Oak Ridge 37830

Tennessee Scenic Riders
Association
P.O. Box 3104
Nashville 37219

Tennessee Valley Canoe Club
Box 11125
Chattanooga 37401

University of Tennessee
Hiking & Canoe Club
Route 6
Concord 37730

Texas
Heart of Texas Canoe Club
Box 844
Temple 76501

Houston Canoe Club
3116 Broadway
Houston 77017

Utah
Wasatch Mountain Club
904 Military Dr.
Salt Lake City 84108

Virginia
Appalachian Transit Authority
11453 Washington Plaza, W
Reston 22070

Blue Ridge Voyageurs
8119 Hillcrest Dr.
Manassas 22110

Coastal Canoeists
309 Mimosa Dr.
Newport News 23606

Washington
Cascave Canoe Club
2333 Harris Ave.
Richland 99352

Paddle Trails Canoe Club
Box 86
Ashford 98304

Seattle Canoe Club
6019 51, NE
Seattle 98115

Spokane Canoe Club
N 10804 Nelson
Spokane 99218

Tri-C Camping Association
17404 8th Ave.
Seattle 98155

Washington Kayak Club
8519 California Ave., SW
Seattle 98116

West Virginia
West Virginia Wildwater
Association
Route 1, Box 97
Ravenswood 26164

Wisconsin
Wisconsin Hoofers Outing
Club
3009 Hermina St.
Madison 53714

Glossary

ABEAM   Position that is at right angle to keel.

ABREAST   Parallel or alongside.

ACID RAIN   Rain contaminated with pollutants.

AFT   Stern or back end of the canoe.

AMIDSHIPS   Halfway from the bow to the stern; middle.

ANCHOR   Device for holding the canoe in one place on the water with the weight on the bottom underwater.

ANCHOR LINE   Rope connecting the boat to the anchor.

ASTERN   Back end of the canoe; direction to the back of the canoe.

ASYMMETRICAL CANOE   Canoe in which the bow section is narrower to the point than the stern section.

BACK STROKE   Reverse paddling stroke that moves canoe backwards.

BACKWATER   Reverse stroke that slows forward progress or reverses the canoe course; reverse current.

BALANCING   Keeping the canoe upright in the water by body motion.

BALLAST   Gear or baggage placed in the canoe bottom for balance.

BEFORE THE WIND   Proceeding with the wind coming from behind.

BENT PADDLE   Paddle designed with blade at angle to shaft.

BLADE   The lower wide section of paddle.

BOW   Front end of the canoe.

BOWMAN   Paddler in bow position.

BOWSTROKE   Paddling in bow position.

BROACHING   Canoe is forced by wave power to turn sideways into wave trough.

BUOYANCY   Floating ability.

CAMOUFLAGE   Painting and decorating canoe and paddlers to hide them from the view of wildlife.

CANOE POLE   Wooden pole used instead of paddle to propel the canoe.

CARTOP CARRIER   Rig for mounting canoe on car roof.

CASUAL RECREATION   A category label for canoe design.

CENTER LINE   The median keel line of canoe.

CENTER OF GRAVITY   Point in canoe where it is balanced.

CLEAT   Device on dock to which line is attached.

COAST GUARD   United States government agency which enforces regulations.

COMPETITION CRUISING   A category label for canoe design.

COURSE   Planned trip outline; direction of travel.

CRASH HELMET   Helmet similar to cycle helmet for white water canoeing.

CROSS TIE   Tiedown pattern for holding canoe off dock or on car top.

CURRENT   Moving water in stream, river, or tide.

DAY TRIPPER   A category label for canoe design.

DECK   Flat covered area at bow and stern of canoe.

DEEP VEE   Sharply cut hull design.

DEPTH   Measurement from keel of canoe to waterline.

DESTINATION   Point accepted as end of trip.

DISEMBARKING   Getting out of the canoe.

DOUBLE PADDLE   Paddle with shaft and two blades at ends.

DOUSING   Getting wet.

DOWNSTREAM   Paddling with the current.

DRY BAG   Plastic bag that keeps contents dry.

DUFFLE   Gear and equipment carried aboard.

ELECTRIC MOTOR   Type used by fishermen for trolling.

EMBARKING   Getting into craft.

FENDING OFF   Keeping craft away from dock, land, or other craft.

FINISHES   Paints or plastics for covering canoe skin.

FIRST AID   Medical equipment aboard; repairing injury.

FISHERMAN'S BEND   Knot used for tying up.

FLARE   The amount of angle upward and outward usually at bow and stern; a light or flame used to attract attention.

FLAT BOTTOM   Bottom of the canoe is flat to the curve of the sides.

FLOTATION   Device and material to keep canoe from sinking full of water.

FOLLOWING SEA   Waves coming in same direction as canoe.

FREIGHT CANOE   Large canoe used by explorers and wilderness travelers to transport goods and heavy equipment.

FULLY FOUND   Canoe and passengers with everything necessary aboard.

GEAR   Equipment and necessities aboard.

GLIDE   Canoe proceeds without power after stroke.

GRIP   Top of paddle; the handle.

GUIDE   One who shows the way.

GUNWALE   Top edge of the canoe.

GRUB   Food.

HAIRPIN TURN   Sudden and sharp turn in canoe course.

HEAD-ON   Directly forward; coming directly at canoe bow.

HULL CONFIGURATION   Dimensions of canoe to specific design.

J-STROKE   Part of forward stroke that corrects canoe direction.

KEEL LINE   The line of the keel.

LAMINATE   Several wood strips glued together.

LANDING   Act of coming ashore and getting out; place to come ashore.

LEAD CANOE   First canoe in a party, group, or fleet.

LEE BOARDS   Wood planks used as keels in sailing canoe.

LENGTH   Measured distance from bow to stern.

LEVERAGE   Amount of effective weight or force to accomplish objective.

LIFE JACKET   Safety garment to keep person afloat in water.

LIFT   Amount of upcurve of bottom line of canoe at ends.

LINE   Bow and stern ropes for tying.

LINING   Bringing canoe around unsafe water with ropes.

LITTERING   Leaving garbage and refuse in water or on land.

MOTOR BRACKET   Device mounted on canoe to hold water.

MOTOR POWER   Power given to canoe by mechanical engine.

NACLO   National Association of Canoe Liveries and Outfitters.

OAR   Two paddle blade on a long shaft used to row canoe.

OARLOCKS   Fulcrum device for holding oar during stroke.

OVERBOARD   Person or gear outside canoe in water.

PACE   Speed of canoe set and regulated; speed of paddle stroke.

PAINTER   Bow rope.

PEAK   The rise of canoe height at both ends.

PFD   Personal flotation device.

PARALLEL   Position similar to or alongside another canoe.

PONTOONS   Flotation devices mounted on each side of canoe for stability.

PORT   Left side of canoe facing forward.

PORTAGE   Carrying canoe from water to water overland.

PORTAGE YOKE   Device mounted on thwart for carrying canoe on shoulders.

RACING   A category of canoe designed for competition.

RAIN GUTTER   Slot in car roof above doors.

RAPIDS   Fast water of stream or tide current.

RIB   Series of vertical wood strips to sustain hull planks.

RIB-STRIP CONSTRUCTION   Vertical wood strips and thin lateral planks that form hull.

RIVER RAT   One who continually is found canoeing on a specific river.

ROCKERED ENDS   Ends of canoe designed to bend upwards from flat keel line.

ROLL BAR   Bar on cartop carrier that revolves so canoe can be rolled on carrier easily.

ROUNDED VEE   Designation for a deep hull design.

ROWING   Act of propelling canoe with oars.

ROWING SEAT   Seat mounted in center of canoe for rowing.

SAILING CANOE   Canoe equipped with sails and rigging.

SCOUTING   Looking forward toward prospective course.

SHAFT   Part of paddle between blade and handle.

SHALLOW   Area in river or lake that is of little depth.

SHALLOW ARCH   Designation of canoe design.

SHALLOW DRAFT   Canoe that takes minimum of water to float it.

SHALLOW VEE   Designation of canoe hull shape.

SHEER LINE   Fore and aft curvature of design.

SHELVING RIFFLE   Area in river where water is shallow on one side.

SHIPPING WATER   Water taken in over the canoe side.

SIDE MOTOR MOUNT   Device mounted on canoe to hold outboard engine.

SILENT STROKE   Paddle stroke in which takeup after stroke is done by knifing paddle through the water.

SNUBBING   Tightening on line or slowing canoe course.

SOLO CANOEING   One paddler canoeing alone.

SPRAY RAIL   Strip on the side of canoe to deflect waves.

SQUALL   Sudden rain and wind storm.

SQUARE STERN   Stern of canoe is straight across for use with motor.

STEM BAND   Outside cover of the bow and stern edge from peak down to keel.

STOP STROKE   Paddle stroke made to stop canoe in water.

STRAIGHT SHAFT PADDLE   Paddle with no angulation.

STROKE   Motion of paddler with paddle to propel canoe.

/ Glossary

SWAMPED   Canoe has been partially submerged in water.

SWEEP STROKE   Forward stroke made in wide circle for fast turn.

SYMMETRICAL   Both ends of canoe are same design in point.

TACKING   Canoeing a course against the wind at an angle.

TAIL CANOE   Last canoe in a party.

TAIL PAD   Seat.

TANDEM CANOE   Canoe designed for two paddlers.

THROAT   Section of paddle above blade.

THWART   Crossbars in canoe for strengthening.

TIEDOWN   Method of tying canoe to dock, car top, or storage area.

TOURING CANOE   Designation of canoe design for distance running.

TUMBLEHOME   Outward curvature or bulge from waterline to gunwale.

TURBULENCE   Disturbed water conditions.

USCA   United States Canoe Association.

VEE HULL   Hull design of sharp deep proportions.

WASH   Area behind rock or passing craft where water is waved and forms a strong force.

WAVE   Water rise caused by wind, wake, or current.

WAVE SURGE   Motion of wave from boat wake, wind, or current.

WET SUIT   Rubber suit worn next to skin for dryness and warmth.

WHITE WATER   River or stream where speed and obstructions cause surflike conditions.

WHITE WATER END CAP   Covering at bow and stern of canoe to fend off water coming in over the top.

WILDERNESS TRIPPING   Hull designation for canoe used for hard and long wilderness travel.

WIDTH   Widest part of the craft.

YOKE   Device mounted on center thwart for carrying canoe on shoulders for portaging.